# ANIMAL FRIENDSHIP! COLLECTION

## NATIONAL GEOGRAPHIC

WASHINGTON, D.C.

# Inside This BOOK

**DON'T MISS:** Funny Animals!

Book 1

# BEST FRIENDS FOREVER!

## And More True Stories of Animal Friendships

Amy Shields

**Published by the National Geographic Society**
John M. Fahey, *Chairman of the Board and Chief Executive Officer*
Declan Moore, *Executive Vice President; President, Publishing and Travel*
Melina Gerosa Bellows, *Executive Vice President; Chief Creative Officer, Books, Kids, and Family*

**Prepared by the Book Division**
Hector Sierra, *Senior Vice President and General Manager*
Nancy Laties Feresten, *Senior Vice President, Kids Publishing and Media*
Jonathan Halling, *Design Director, Books and Children's Publishing*
Jay Sumner, *Director of Photography, Children's Publishing*
Jennifer Emmett, *Vice President, Editorial Director, Children's Books*
Eva Absher-Schantz, *Design Director, Kids Publishing and Media*
R. Gary Colbert, *Production Director*
Jennifer A. Thornton, *Director of Managing Editorial*

**Staff for This Book**
Marfé Ferguson Delano, *Project Editor*
Becky Baines, *Editor*
Lisa Jewell, *Illustrations Editor*
David Seager, *Art Director*
Ruthie Thompson, *Designer*
Grace Hill and Michael O'Connor, *Associate Managing Editors*
Joan Gossett, *Production Editor*
Lewis R. Bassford, *Production Manager*
Susan Borke, *Legal and Business Affairs*
Ariane Szu-Tu, *Editorial Assistant*
Callie Broaddus, *Design Production Assistant*
Hillary Moloney, *Illustrations Assistant*

**Manufacturing and Quality Management**
Phillip L. Schlosser, *Senior Vice President*
Chris Brown, *Vice President, NG Book Manufacturing*
George Bounelis, *Vice President, Production Services*
Nicole Elliott, *Manager*
Rachel Faulise, *Manager*
Robert L. Barr, *Manager*

The National Geographic Society is one of the world's largest nonprofit scientific and educational organizations. Founded in 1888 to "increase and diffuse geographic knowledge," the Society's mission is to inspire people to care about the planet. It reaches more than 400 million people worldwide each month through its official journal, *National Geographic,* and other magazines; National Geographic Channel; television documentaries; music; radio; films; books; DVDs; maps; exhibitions; live events; school publishing programs; interactive media; and merchandise. National Geographic has funded more than 10,000 scientific research, conservation, and exploration projects and supports an education program promoting geographic literacy.

For more information, please visit www.nationalgeographic.com, call 1-800-NGS LINE (647-5463), or write to the following address:
National Geographic Society
1145 17th Street N.W.
Washington, D.C. 20036-4688 U.S.A.

Visit us online at
www.nationalgeographic.com/books

For librarians and teachers:
www.ngchildrensbooks.org

National Geographic supports K–12 educators with ELA Common Core Resources. Visit natgeoed.org/commoncore for more information.

More for kids from National Geographic:
kids.nationalgeographic.com

For information about special discounts for bulk purchases, please contact National Geographic Books Special Sales: ngspecsales@ngs.org

For rights or permissions inquiries, please contact National Geographic Books Subsidiary Rights: ngbookrights@ngs.org

Trade paperback
ISBN: 978-1-4263-0935-9
Reinforced library edition
ISBN: 978-1-4263-0954-0

Printed in China
14/RRDS/1

# Table of CONTENTS

# ROSCOE AND SURYIA: BEST FRIENDS FOREVER

It was love at first sight when Suryia the orangutan met this dog named Roscoe.

Bubbles gives a lift to Suryia, Roscoe, and animal trainer Moksha Bybee.

## Chapter 1

# The BEST DAY Ever

**Summer 2008,
Myrtle Beach, South Carolina**

It was a muggy, hot day. An elephant named Bubbles strolled through the woods. On her back bounced a fuzzy-haired orangutan named Suryia (sounds like SUR-ee-uh). Bubbles and Suryia were excited. They knew there was a river at the end of the path. Soon they were going to be *in* that river. They were going for a swim!

A man named Doc walked beside Bubbles and Suryia. Looking ahead, he saw a hound dog. It sat alone on the riverbank. It looked like a hungry dog. It was so skinny you could see its ribs. Just then, Suryia spied the dog, too. Before Doc could stop him, the playful ape jumped off Bubbles.

Suryia ran to the dog. He threw his long, hairy arms around it. *Uh-oh,* thought Doc. *A hungry dog might be a mean dog.*

## Did You Know?

**Orangutans eat mostly fruit, nuts, and tree bark. Their favorite food is a stinky fruit called durian (sounds like DUR-ee-ann).**

But the dog didn't mind a big, hairy hug. He even wagged his tail. Then he pounced at Suryia. The seven-year-old orangutan pounced back. That was their I-like-you, do-you-like-me? moment. The answer was yes!

The new pals chased each other in circles. Then they flopped down to rest. The orangutan put his arm around the dog. He pulled him close. They acted "like long lost friends," Doc said.

After a while it was time to leave. Doc lifted Suryia back onto Bubbles. He tried to send the dog back to its own home.

But the dog followed them. He wagged his tail all the way. Wherever Suryia was, that's where the dog wanted to be. "I guess you've decided to stay," said Doc. He named the dog Roscoe.

Doc is Dr. Bhagavan Antle (sounds like BAG-uh-vahn ANN-tuhl). He is the director of a wildlife preserve in Myrtle Beach, South Carolina. Suryia and Bubbles are just two of the animals that live there.

Doc and the other caregivers at the preserve also look after lions and tigers. They care for leopards and cheetahs. They watch over monkeys, chimpanzees, and other orangutans like Suryia. There's even a liger (sounds like LIE-ger) named Hercules at the preserve. A liger is the cub of a lion father and a tiger mother.

Now Doc had a new animal to take care of, and Suryia had a new best friend.

Roscoe is a bluetick coonhound. Blueticks are smart and friendly. They really like to hunt. Blueticks keep their noses to the ground, sniffing for clues. They forget everything except *Find it, find it!*

# Island Homes

Orangutans used to live everywhere in Asia. Today they live in the wild on only two small islands. These are Sumatra (sounds like sue-MAH-tra) and Borneo (sounds like BORE-nee-oh).

Wild orangutans make their homes in rain forests. Farmers and loggers are cutting down the forests on these islands. They want to make palm tree farms. This leaves orangutans with even fewer places to live. It is harder for them to find food. Unless their forest homes are protected, there will soon be no more wild orangutans.

A bluetick coonhound won't stop until it catches its prey or chases it up a tree.

Roscoe might have been hunting the day he met Suryia. Maybe he went too far. Maybe he could not find his way back home. Maybe he did not have a home.

At first, Doc kept a careful eye on Suryia and Roscoe. Animals often get scared when something new enters their world. Suryia had never been face-to-face with a dog before. Had Roscoe ever met an orangutan? Not likely!

Scared dogs growl. They show their teeth. Their ears go back. The hair on their back stands straight up. When orangutans get scared, they look like they're smiling. A silly grin on their face means they're shaking inside. Doc never saw anything like that on Suryia's face. And Roscoe never growled. He never showed other signs of fear, either. Not even once.

Since the day they met, it's been Suryia and Roscoe, best friends forever. Neither one is the boss. If Roscoe wants to nap, Suryia flops down beside him. If Suryia lies down to rest, Roscoe does, too.

Suryia is better at sharing than Roscoe, however. Suryia shares everything. He breaks up his cookies and feeds pieces to Roscoe. Roscoe really likes Suryia's special monkey cookies.

Suryia also tries to share bananas with Roscoe. Roscoe does *not* like bananas. He will not open his mouth. He turns his face away. Then Suryia gives up. He eats the banana himself. Suryia loves bananas.

Best buds since the day they met, Suryia and Roscoe enjoy cuddling up with each other.

## Chapter 2

# Ambassador SURYIA

Suryia has a special job at the animal preserve. He is one of Doc's "animal ambassadors" (sounds like am-BASS-uh-ders). The word "ambassador" usually means a person who represents his or her country. Suryia's job is to represent orangutans that live in the rain forests.

Doc thinks it's good for people to see Suryia and the other animals at the preserve up close. He wants people to see them in action. He hopes this will make people want to help protect the animals' relatives in the wild.

Suryia is a great animal ambassador. People just love to watch him. When Suryia and Roscoe are together, they really draw a crowd!

Sometimes the two friends walk in the yard together. Suryia grabs Roscoe's leash and tugs it. That gets his pal going. They stroll around for a few minutes. Soon Suryia does more than just walk. He grabs his feet and rounds himself into a ball. Over and over he rolls. He falls on Roscoe. Then Roscoe jumps on top of him. Suryia pulls the leash one way. Roscoe tugs it back the other way. There is no such thing as walking in a straight line for these two.

Suryia can have fun with almost anything. For him, an empty box is a fine place to sit. Then he puts the box on his head like a hat. It gets a little ripped. That makes it into a good superhero cape! Soon the box is completely torn open. Now Suryia crawls under it. Does anyone want to play hide-and-seek?

Like all orangutans, Suryia likes to make faces. He pulls his bottom lip out. He puckers his rubbery lips. He makes silly smiles. He sticks out his tongue. He wipes his face down with his hand and plays peek-a-boo. Sometimes he blows *pfffffft* sounds. That always makes people laugh.

People don't get tired of watching Suryia. But Suryia does get tired of watching people. He would rather play with Roscoe. He likes to hang out with other orangutans, too.

Lucky Suryia! One of his other jobs is doing exactly that—hanging out with other orangutans. Or really, to let them hang out with him. In the wild, baby orangutans learn about life from their families. At they preserve, they learn from Suryia. They learn by watching and playing with him.

If Suryia lived in the wild, he'd be on his own by now. At the preserve he lives in a house with three younger orangutans. An animal trainer named Moksha Bybee (sounds like MOKE-shuh BYE-bee) lives with them.

Suryia and the three little orangutans love to wrestle. They have fun tickling each other. They run and roll across the yard. Sometimes Suryia grabs a twig to scratch his back. The little ones find their own twigs. They try to scratch their backs. Sometimes Suryia makes kiss-kiss noises at the babies. They make kiss-kiss noises back.

Most of the time Suryia gets along just fine with the little orangutans. But at mealtimes he has to eat by himself. Otherwise, Suryia would grab their food. That's just what older orangutans do.

In the evening, Moksha gives the orangutans a bath. She puts them in the tub. She tries to wash them. They just want to splash. They want to play. This surprises Moksha. In the wild, orangutans do not like water. In the wild, water means danger. In the tub, water means fun.

Lots of things would be different for Suryia if he lived in the wild. At the preserve, he spends his days with lots of other animals. In the rain forest, he would spend his days alone. He would look for food alone. At night he would make a nest of leaves in a treetop and sleep alone. He would not have a dog as a friend!

At the preserve, Moksha helps the young orangutans get ready for bedtime. She pulls blankets into round, soft nests for them. Suryia makes his blanket nest all by himself.

Before lights out, Moksha does one more thing. She calls, "Roscoe, bedtime!" Roscoe runs into the house. Then he curls up to sleep next to his best friend, Suryia.

# Orangutan School

In Sumatra and Borneo, wildlife workers run special schools for young orangutans that don't have moms. The workers teach them skills they need to survive in the wild.

Wild orangutans live in trees. They can go for weeks without touching the ground. At orangutan school, baby orangutans practice on jungle gyms made of ropes and netting. They learn how to climb up and stay up. If a baby goes too high and gets scared, a worker helps it back down. After a cuddle, it's time for another try!

Suryia hitches a ride around the pool from Roscoe. The dog doesn't mind, and Suryia loves it!

**Chapter 3**

# SWIM Buddies

**N**othing beats a swim on a hot summer's day, right? How about going swimming with your best friend? Even better!

Orangutans are not natural-born swimmers. Rivers in their jungle homes can be dangerous places. If a river is flowing fast, an orangutan that falls in might get swept away.

But Suryia doesn't live in the wild. And Moksha knew how much

Suryia loved being in the bathtub. *Hmmm,* thought Moksha. *I wonder if Suryia would like to learn how to swim?*

When Moksha told Doc her idea, he told her to give it a try. So, one day she strapped a life vest on Suryia. She took him to one of the pools on the preserve. It was time for a swimming lesson.

Into the water they went. At first Suryia clung to the side of the pool. He curled the fingers of one hand tightly over the edge. Moksha stood in the water a few steps away from him.

"Come on, Suryia!" she shouted. "Swim to me!" Suryia reached out to Moksha. Looking at her, he let go of the edge. His long arms stretched out and pulled him through the water. Suryia was swimming!

Now Suryia loves to swim. He still needs a life vest. That's because he doesn't quite understand how to cup his hands. So it's hard to get a good pull. Plus, orangutans have very solid, or dense (sounds like DENTS), bodies. That makes it nearly impossible for them to float.

Like many hunting dogs, Roscoe is a great swimmer. Sometimes Suryia holds Roscoe's tail and gets a ride around the pool. *Whee!*

When Moksha taught Suryia to swim, she watched him very closely to see how he was feeling. His body language helps him communicate.

# Swinging Swimmers

In 2009, some orangutans in Borneo did something very surprising. They took a swim. They dropped into the river from branches above. They splashed around. It was like a pool party! Scientists were amazed. No one had ever seen a wild orangutan swim before. The story made the news around the world.

The orangutans were at a rescue center. Scientists think they felt safe. They may have noticed there were no crocodiles in the area. The orangutans searched for food in the water. They also ate fish. And they drank from cup-shaped rocks. Amazing!

If Suryia pulls his lips back to show his teeth, that means he's feeling scared or angry. Moksha saw that look once or twice at the start of the swim lessons. When he opens his mouth but doesn't show any teeth, he's ready to play. A sideways look says, "Calm down. Stop moving." Roscoe gets that sideways look a lot from Suryia.

Doc, Suryia, and Bubbles still go down to the river to swim. Only now, Roscoe rides on top of Bubbles with Suryia. When they head for the path through the woods, both Suryia and Roscoe get excited. They know where they're going! Suryia claps his hands, and Roscoe lets loose with a howl. *Aaah-roooo! How great is this?* he seems to say. *I'm going swimming with my best friend ever!*

Ever since she was a baby, Koko the gorilla has loved cats. Here she is with Tiger.

# KOKO: CRAZY FOR CATS!

Koko is not just big, she is beautiful! She is also smart and loving. You can see it in her eyes.

# Worst Present EVER

## December 1983, Woodside, California

It was Christmas morning. Twelve-year-old Koko had presents to open. First the gorilla looked in her stocking. She found some nuts in it. Koko loved nuts. But this morning, she tossed them aside. Then she unwrapped a doll. "That stink," she told her friend Penny.

Next came a toy cat made of cement. It was covered with black velvet. "That *red!*" Koko exclaimed. Red is not a good thing. When Koko uses the word "red" like that, it means she's angry.

*Uh-oh.* Penny knew Koko wanted a cat. She bought one that could stand up to rough gorilla play. She thought the cement cat was a good present. Koko let Penny know she was wrong. Penny understood. *Koko wants a* real *cat.*

Wait a minute—how could a gorilla tell a human how she felt?

Koko isn't just any gorilla. She's an *amazing* gorilla. She can communicate with American Sign Language, called ASL for short.

ASL is not a spoken language. With ASL you make words with your hands, face, and body. Many people who cannot hear use ASL to speak without sound.

Imagine you are with Koko right now. If you knew ASL you could ask her, "Who are you?" She might sign back, "Fine person gorilla me."

How did Koko learn sign language? Around the time Koko was born, Penny Patterson was a student at Stanford University. She heard scientists Allen and Beatrix Gardner speak about an amazing project. They had taught ASL to a chimpanzee named Washoe (sounds like WASH-oh). Washoe was the first non-human ever to learn how to use ASL. She learned 350 signs.

# Koko's Special Signs

People around the world use different kinds of sign language. In China, people use Chinese Sign Language. They would not understand American Sign Language. And people who use ASL may not understand Gorilla Sign Language.

Koko has smaller thumbs than a human does. This means she can't make some ASL signs. So Koko makes up her own signs. She signs "zebra" as "white tiger." A mask is "eye hat." A ring is "finger bracelet." Koko can be very creative!

Penny decided she wanted to teach an ape to communicate with ASL. Maybe she could find a chimpanzee to teach.

As it turns out, she got a gorilla— Koko! Gorillas and chimpanzees are both in the Great Ape family. They are alike in many ways. Both are very smart.

Koko was born at the San Francisco Zoo on July 4, 1971. When Koko was a year old, Penny talked with the director of the zoo. She asked if she could teach Koko. Penny promised to stay with Koko for four years.

Guess how long Penny stayed with Koko? It's been more than 40 years now! Penny is still Koko's friend and teacher. But now Penny gives better presents. The next present she gave Koko was much better.

Koko cuddles All Ball, her first real kitten. Koko loved to stroke All Ball's head with her finger.

## Chapter 2

# A KITTEN TO LOVE

A few months after that disappointing Christmas, Penny decided to get Koko a real cat. She was as sure as she could be that Koko would not hurt a kitten. After all, Koko loved cats. Her favorite stories were "Puss in Boots" and "The Three Little Kittens."

One day Penny heard about three kittens that had lost their

mother. Penny had them brought to the Gorilla Foundation, in Woodside, California. She and Koko live there in side-by-side houses.

Penny took the kittens to meet Koko. One was brown, and two were gray. One of the gray ones had no tail. Koko signed, "Love that," when she saw the kittens.

Penny told Koko she could choose one kitten. Koko picked them up one by one. She looked in their eyes. She blew in their faces. She does this when she meets a new animal or person. Then she chose the gray kitten with no tail. "Koko love," she signed.

"What will you name the kitty?" Penny asked.

"All Ball," Koko signed. With no tail, it really did look like a ball of soft gray fur.

Koko tucked All Ball's tiny gray head against her big furry belly. She was very gentle with All Ball. She treated him like a baby. A gorilla baby. Koko pushed All Ball up on her back. Mother gorillas carry their babies on their backs.

All Ball climbed all over Koko. Sometimes the little kitten used his sharp claws to climb. *Ouch!* Koko signed, "Cat do scratch."

All Ball turned out to be a little rowdy. It might be because he was orphaned when he was still young. He had no mother to teach him to be gentle. Sometimes All Ball bit Koko. "Cat bite. Obnoxious," Koko signed. Did Koko ever scratch or bite back? Nope. She was patient with her new little friend.

Koko liked to groom All Ball. She combed his hair. She petted him. Every day she looked carefully into his eyes, ears, and mouth to make sure everything was all right. What a good friend!

Koko liked to talk about All Ball. She had many conversations with Barbara Hiller. Barbara was a co-founder with Penny of the Gorilla Foundation. When Barbara asked Koko to tell about All Ball she signed, "Soft."

"Do you love All Ball?" Barbara asked.

"Soft good cat cat," signed Koko.

Koko loving All Ball? No problem. Koko playing with him? That could be a *big* problem. At the time, Koko weighed

200 pounds (91 kg) and stood 5 feet (152 cm) tall. All Ball weighed 6 ounces (.17 kg) and was 4 inches (10 cm) tall. That's like you playing with a butterfly. When Koko and All Ball were lying on the floor, Koko would sign, "Tickle." Koko loves being tickled. If All Ball knew what "tickle" meant, he would have said, "No way!" All Ball did *not* like to be tickled.

So Penny helped Koko pretend that All Ball was playing tickle. Penny held All Ball in one hand and tickled Koko with the other. That worked. Koko thought this was a funny idea. "Huh, huh, huh," laughed Koko, as she pretended to be tickled by her pal.

Another favorite Koko game is chase. Can you imagine a game of chase between a gorilla and a kitten? Cats like to be the chaser. So does Koko. Koko tried to chase All Ball. But the kitten stood still and arched his back. That was OK with Koko. Nothing about All Ball made Koko mad or sad.

Then one day something awful happened. All Ball slipped out the door. He ran into the road, and a car hit him.

Penny told Koko about the accident. Koko did not say anything. At first Penny thought she did not understand. But when she closed the door to Koko's home, she heard Koko start to hoot, soft and sad. Penny cried, too. Koko was crying for her friend All Ball. Penny was crying for All Ball and Koko.

# Gentle Giants

There are two kinds of gorillas. Mountain gorillas live in forests in the eastern part of Africa. Lowland gorillas roam forests in western Africa. Koko is a lowland gorilla. Free-living gorillas chow down on wild celery and roots. They munch on fruit and bamboo shoots. They also eat tree bark and pulp.

Gorillas may look a little scary. But most of the time they are gentle and peaceful. They share their food. They protect their babies. They can feel happy or sad. Just like humans.

Climbing onto Koko's head is like reaching a mountaintop for Smoky the kitten.

## Chapter 3

# SORRY, Koko Love Good

Three days went by before Penny asked Koko about All Ball. She asked, "Do you want to talk about your kitty?" Koko signed, "Cry." Then she signed, "Want."

Penny asked if Koko could say what happened. Koko signed, "Sleep cat." Penny asked how Koko felt. Koko signed, "Bad, sorry, Koko love good."

Another time Koko saw a picture of a kitten that looked a lot like All Ball. She pointed to the picture and signed, "Cry, sad, frown." She put her finger to her eye to show the path of a tear. She pulled her bottom lip down to sign "frown." This was a very sad time for Koko. It hurts to lose someone you love.

Penny decided to get a new kitten for Koko. She found a family with a kitten to share. They brought it to Koko in a box.

*What? Only one kitten?* Koko pointed to the box. She signed, "Pick there."

Koko wanted to choose her own cat. Now she got grumpy. "Think fake look," she signed to Penny. She didn't get to see two or three kittens rolling around. It *was* a fake look!

The new kitten was orange with a bright pink nose. Koko named him Lips Lipstick. Penny thinks its pink nose made Koko think of lipstick. Koko played with Lips, but she just didn't seem to love this kitty the way she loved All Ball. Somebody else did, though.

Michael was another gorilla at the Gorilla Foundation. He was also learning sign language from Penny and other staff members. It's a good thing Koko had Michael as a playmate. When a gorilla wants to have wild crazy fun, only another gorilla can keep up! These two romped like brother and sister.

Just like a brother and sister, if Koko had a cat, Michael wanted a cat. He called Lips "my cat red." Since Michael seemed to care more about Lips than Koko did, Penny gave the kitty to him.

For her next kitten, Koko had a choice. Penny brought her two kittens. One was black and white. Koko petted it first. But when she lifted it out of the box, it ran away. Koko caught the kitten. Then she signed, "Baby, baby, baby obnoxious, darn."

The other kitten was gray. This one ran right into Koko's lap. Koko said, "Mine Koko love." Koko kissed the kitty and walked a few steps away. The kitten followed her. "Love," signed Koko, cradling the kitten. Then she showed the kitten her favorite doll. Koko placed a bead necklace around the kitten's neck. This one was a keeper.

A few days later Penny asked Koko if she had named her new friend yet. "That smoke," said Koko. And Smoky was its name.

Over the years, other cats have come to live at the Gorilla Foundation. But these days Koko has a new interest: babies. Not human babies, gorilla babies. She has a special gorilla friend named Ndume (sounds like en-DOO-may). Ndume is male. Penny and the other scientists at the Gorilla Foundation hope Koko and Ndume will have babies together.

If Koko does have a baby, will she teach it to sign? Penny thinks she might. When Koko plays with her dolls, she moves their arms and pretends they are signing. Maybe she's just practicing until she has a real, live baby to teach.

## Naughty Name Callers

Just like humans, Michael and Koko found it hard to be on their best behavior all the time. One time Michael misbehaved. Penny had to scold him and remind him to be a good gorilla. She could hear Koko making a "huh, huh, huh" sound. Koko thought it was funny that Michael got in trouble.

Another time Michael and Koko called each other names. Koko called Michael "Stupid toilet." Michael called Koko "Stink bad squash gorilla." Those were big naughty words, and they both knew it!

In the meantime, Koko has plenty to keep her busy. She works with Penny and plays with Ndume. She uses more than 1,000 ASL signs. She enjoys drinking tea and looking at magazines. She also teaches Penny and other Gorilla Foundation scientists something new every day.

In November 2011, Koko picked two new friends from a litter of kittens. One had stripes like a tiger. The other was all black. What do you think Koko named them? Tiger and Blackie! Koko is a good friend to them. She tucks them in her nest of blankets. She boosts them up on her shoulders. She cradles them in her arms. Clever Koko picked two kittens who like being friends with a gorilla. Koko is still crazy for cats!

# JASMINE: SUPER-FRIEND!

Jasmine the greyhound snuggles with some of her friends. Which one thinks she's a *hoot* to play with?

Jasmine and her fox friend Roxy are all set for a stroll in the park.

# LEARNING TO TRUST

## Nuneaton, England, 2003

Inside a dark garden shed, a young dog whimpered. She was all alone. She was very hungry and very scared. Someone had locked her in the shed and just left her there. Day after day passed. No one came to feed her or check on her. She grew weaker and weaker.

It's a good thing some police officers found the dog before it was too late. They could tell she needed special care to get better. So they took the dog to a person named Geoff (sounds like JEFF) Grewcock.

Geoff lives in England in a town called Nuneaton (sounds like nun-EE-ton). He has a soft spot in his heart for every animal in need. In 2001 he set up an animal sanctuary (sounds like SANK-choo-air-ee) in his own home to help them. It's a place where he and other volunteers care for animals that are sick or hurt or have lost their mothers. Once the animals can survive on their own, they are released back into the wild.

The dog the police brought to Geoff was not a wild animal. But she sure needed help. Her eyes were dull. Her skin lay on her ribs like a thin blanket. As soon as Geoff saw her, he knew he had to help her.

Geoff named the dog Jasmine (sounds like JAZZ-men). She was a greyhound. In some places, greyhounds are bred to race on a track. Dog racing is a popular sport. But when a dog starts to lose races, some heartless dog owners don't want to feed or care for them anymore. Geoff thinks that may be what happened to Jasmine.

Geoff and his co-workers nursed Jasmine back to health. They also tried to win her trust. Sudden movements and loud noises scared her. So everyone moved slowly. They tried to talk quietly. In time, Jasmine learned to trust them. After several weeks of special care and good food, she grew healthy and happy.

Geoff started to look for someone to adopt Jasmine. He wanted to find a nice family to love her and take care of her.

In the meantime, Jasmine found her own place. It was on the couch in the sanctuary office.

Every time someone brought in a box or a cage, Jasmine looked up. Then she unfolded her long legs and stepped down from the couch. She poked her long nose inside the box. She sniffed at whatever animal had been brought in for help. Then she gave it a gentle lick. Geoff thought Jasmine was telling the animals, "Don't worry. You're safe now."

Jasmine licked fox and badger cubs. She licked rabbits. "She even let the birds perch on the bridge of her nose," Geoff says.

Soon Jasmine became the official greeter at the sanctuary. "She seemed to have a need to comfort every creature, great and small," Geoff recalls. So many helpless animals needed a friend like Jasmine! She welcomed owls, swans, hedgehogs, and many others to the sanctuary. After a while, Geoff decided the sanctuary needed Jasmine. So he adopted her.

One day, Geoff got a call from the local train station. Two newborn puppies had been found on the tracks. Could Geoff come and get them?

Geoff jumped into his car. On the way back with the puppies, he wondered what Jasmine would do. He knew she had never had puppies of her own. Would she know how to help these newborns?

As soon as Geoff brought the puppies in, Jasmine leaped off the couch. With her mouth, she picked one puppy up by the scruff of his neck. She carried him to the couch. She went back for the other pup. Then she jumped onto the couch herself. She tucked those babies close to her tummy and curled around them. Somehow, she knew they needed more than a lick.

When Geoff came back with bottles of warm goat's milk, Jasmine nudged the puppies awake. After feeding them, Geoff returned the pups to Jasmine. She licked them clean and settled them in for another nap. *That went well,* thought Geoff. He smiled at Jasmine and the puppies.

## Built for Speed

Greyhounds are one of the oldest dog breeds. Ancient Egyptians hunted with them nearly 3,000 years ago. Tomb carvings show the dogs chasing deer and mountain goats. They were brought to England more than 1,000 years ago. Greyhounds are the second fastest land animals. Only cheetahs are swifter. With their long legs and lean bodies, greyhounds can run like the wind. In races, they have been clocked at 45 miles (72 km) an hour!

Bramble looks lively here, but the fawn was very sick when he first came to the animal sanctuary.

## Chapter 2

# A FAWN IN NEED

Geoff named the puppies Buster and Toby. Both of them were terriers (sounds like TER-ee-ers). And both did just fine, thanks to Jasmine. Geoff thinks she might have saved their lives.

That's because Jasmine was more than just a good friend to Buster and Toby. By keeping them safe and warm with her body, she also acted like a mother dog to the little puppies when they needed it most.

Another time someone dropped off a very small, very weak fox cub at the sanctuary. Jasmine knew what a mom would do. With Geoff and Jasmine's help, the fox cub grew lively and strong. Geoff named her Roxy. Roxy and Jasmine became great friends. They liked going on walks together.

Soon another animal needed Jasmine's special touch. It was a tiny baby deer, or fawn. Two people hiking through the woods found it lying out in the open. It was right next to the path. Normally, mother deer keep their babies hidden. The hikers could tell right away that this fawn was in trouble. At first they wondered, *Is it even breathing?* Then they saw it was alive. But they knew it couldn't survive by itself.

The hikers lifted the fawn and carried him to their car. They took him to a veterinarian (sounds like vet-er-ih-NARE-ee-en). The vet thought the fawn was about two weeks old. He also thought there was no hope for it. "He's too far gone," the vet said. "He can't be saved." But the people who found him wouldn't give up.

They drove on until they reached the wildlife sanctuary. "Can you help, please?" they asked Stacey Clarke. Stacey works at the sanctuary with Geoff. The people told Stacey the vet thought the fawn would die. Stacey didn't say so, but she agreed with the vet. The fawn had been alone and without food for far too long. But she agreed to try.

In the end, however, it was Jasmine who kept the fawn alive.

She had a little help from Geoff and Stacey, of course. They fed the fawn bottles of warm goat's milk every three to four hours. Then Jasmine took over. She seemed to sense that the fawn not only needed a friend. He also needed some mothering. Jasmine was just the dog to give it to him. She licked and cleaned the fawn. She snuggled with him on the couch and kept him warm. Day by day, the fawn grew stronger. Finally, he was out of danger. When Geoff was sure that the fawn was going to make it, he named him Bramble.

When Bramble grew strong enough, he and Jasmine went for walks together. Sometimes a chipmunk surprised them, or a loud bird cried nearby. Then Bramble hid underneath Jasmine.

Bramble stuck to Jasmine like glue. "Bramble walked between her legs and they kept kissing each other," Geoff recalls. "They walked together round the sanctuary. It was a real treat to see them."

Bramble often checked with Jasmine by putting his nose to her nose. Deer have an excellent sense of smell. In the wild, Bramble would have touched noses with his mother often during the day. He would have learned, by the way his mother's nose smelled, if a place or another animal was safe. He might have been trying this with Jasmine.

**Did You Know?**

A dog can get very sick from eating chocolate, grapes, or raisins.

## Fast Friends

Greyhounds only race until they are three or four years old. Then they retire from the track. Many groups try to find forever homes for former race dogs. One of them, called Adopt-A-Greyhound, says, "We'd like to introduce you to the fastest friend you'll ever meet!"

Adopt-A-Greyhound helps people turn racing dogs into pets. Life in a house is different than life at the racetrack. For example, the dogs need to be taught how to walk up and down stairs. That's something they never had to do when they were racers.

Seeing Bramble and Jasmine together surprised visitors. Why would a dog and a deer become such good friends? It had a lot to do with Bramble's age. Scientists say very young animals are up for anything. They don't know if something is weird. Their motto seems to be, "If it feels good, do it!"

Also, living at the sanctuary makes odd friendships possible. After all, none of the animals has to worry about food. They know that Geoff and Stacey will feed them. In the wild, a hungry fox might gobble up a duckling. In the sanctuary, the rattle of plastic dishes filled with kibble and meat is what makes them hungry, not their little duck friend.

Jasmine and Bramble were lucky to have found each other.

Bramble stretches his head up to touch noses with his best friend, Jasmine.

# ONE OF A KIND

Geoff thinks there could be another reason for Jasmine and Bramble's strong friendship. They kind of looked alike. They both had long legs. They both had pointy faces with long noses. They both had big brown eyes and small delicate ears. They even had the same fur color. Bramble might have thought, *Are you my mother?*

It wasn't long before Bramble grew too big to snuggle with Jasmine on the couch. Soon he was old enough to release into the wild. But there was a problem. Bramble had been at the sanctuary for several months. That was long enough for him to think of Geoff and Stacey as his friends. In the woods, he wouldn't last long if he thought every person he met was his friend.

Geoff also thought that separating Jasmine and Bramble would be mean. The greyhound and deer didn't spend all their time together anymore. But when Jasmine came out of the office, she always looked for Bramble. They still loved to walk together. Bramble might run off to check out a noise, but he always came back to Jasmine's side. They rubbed their cheeks together. They leaned on each other. They were such good friends.

So Bramble ended up staying. Jasmine continued to welcome new animals in the office. Bramble also made some new friends. He met a badger named Humbug. He hung out with a big buzzard named Ellie. He took walks with Roxy the fox.

Bramble really hit it off with a turkey named Tinsel. Nobody knows how the two animals got together. It could be that Bramble just liked what was in Tinsel's dinner bowl. Maybe he decided to stick around for more.

Now, Bramble curls up in the barn to sleep with Tinsel every night. Tinsel pecks at Bramble's face. When he gobbles, Bramble comes around to see what's up.

Jasmine used to visit Bramble and Tinsel in the barn. She would lick Bramble's face and stay with them for a while. Jasmine's life at the sanctuary was very happy. She loved everybody, and they loved her. So it was sad when she passed away from old age in 2011. Geoff isn't sure exactly how old Jasmine was. He does know that she made the world a better place, one animal orphan at a time. Today her spot on the couch is sometimes taken by a new puppy or fox cub. But there will never be another Jasmine, Geoff says. The gentle greyhound was one of a kind. Jasmine was a best friend to all.

# Deer Details

Deer live on every continent except Antarctica. They make their home in woodlands, forests, and mountains. They are also found in deserts and grasslands. There are more than 43 different kinds of deer.

Bramble is a roe deer. Roe deer live in England and other parts of Europe. In North America, most deer are white-tailed deer. Roe deer are about half as big as white-tailed deer. Roe deer and white-tailed deer both have reddish fur in the summer. In winter their fur turns gray.

Owen the hippo follows Mzee the tortoise wherever he goes.

# OWEN AND MZEE: ODD COUPLE

Owen is about one year old in this picture. At the time, the cute little hippo weighed about 600 pounds (272 kg).

# Chapter 1

# Little Lost HIPPO

## December 2003, Malindi, Kenya

On Christmas Day the beach in Malindi (sounds like ma-LIN-dee), Kenya, was crowded. Usually people on a beach watch the waves. Not today on this beach! Everybody was looking at a group of hippopotamuses, or hippos.

The hippos had appeared on the beach a few days earlier. Before that, they had lived in a river many miles away. Then heavy rains came and flooded the river. The fast-moving water washed the hippos downstream. They ended up at the beach.

The Malindi beach is popular with tourists. The white sand and turquoise-blue ocean are two reasons why people want to go to there. A third reason is that you can see a lot of fantastic animals nearby. Kenya, a country on the east coast of Africa, is home to elephants, eagles, giraffes, zebras, and more.

The tourists probably thought it was exciting to have the hippos on the beach. The villagers knew better. Even from a distance, the adult hippos looked big and strong. There was a calf, or baby, too. The adults would try to protect it. Hippos can be dangerous to people. And the ocean can be dangerous for hippos. They can't swim in the ocean.

That night many people went to bed thinking about the hippos. By morning, there was something else to worry about.

Early in the morning on December 26, 2004, an underwater earthquake exploded in the Indian Ocean. It was the third strongest earthquake in history. It triggered a series of massive waves. The giant waves wiped out beaches and towns in Indonesia. Many people were hurt or killed. That evening, the waves hit the coast of Kenya. They weren't as big by then, but they were still big enough to cause damage.

# River Horses

Hippopotamus means "river horse" in ancient Greek. Hippos live in Africa. The sun there is strong and hot. Water keeps the hippos cool. Being underwater protects them from sunburn. They even nap in the water. They lift their noses out just enough to get a breath, but not enough to wake themselves up!

Hippos can't really swim. Their bodies are too heavy. They move through the water by sinking to the river bottom. Then they push off with their legs.

The next day, people came out to see the Malindi beach. Boats had been thrown up on the shore. Beach chairs were bobbing in the ocean. And the hippos? There was only one left—the calf. People did not know what happened to the others. One thing was certain. The calf needed to be rescued.

First, they needed to catch it. Fishermen unrolled their big nets. Moving in a line, they held the nets in front of them. They inched toward the hippo. Villagers and tourists helped. But hippos are fast. They're slippery, too, and big. This little baby weighed about 600 pounds (272 kg)! Again and again the people chased him. No luck. When they zigged, he zagged.

The hippo calf ran back and forth on the reef for hours. Finally, the rescuers trapped him in a net. Everyone cheered! But then the calf kicked and twisted. He broke the net that held him. He got loose again. The rescuers were exhausted, but they were determined. They traded their fishing nets for shark nets. Shark nets are much stronger.

Finally, a visitor named Owen Sobien tackled the hippo. Owen played rugby at home in France, so he knew how to tackle! Everyone quickly threw their nets over the hippo. They pinned him down. Caught! Hundreds of people cheered. They clapped and whistled. What a relief! Someone thought to call the nearest wildlife sanctuary, Haller Park. It's near Mombasa (sounds like mom-BAH-sah), a town about 50 miles (80 km) down the coast.

Dr. Paula Kahumbu (ka-HUM-boo) was the manager at Haller Park. She knew that if they didn't go get the hippo, he had no chance at all. She asked Stephen Tuei (too-WAY) to go with her. He is the chief animal caretaker at Haller Park.

Paula and Stephen jumped in her truck. When they got to Malindi, they saw the calf. He was tied up, lying on his side in the back of a truck. The hippo was breathing hard. He had cuts and scratches from the reef. He had a sunburn. But he was alive.

Paula asked the rescuers if they had named the hippo calf. They hadn't yet. People called out ideas. Finally, everyone started yelling, "Owen! Owen!" They named the hippo after the brave man who tackled him.

Owen wants to play, so he nudges Mzee to wake him. Mzee moves on turtle time— slow and steady.

## Chapter 2

# A NEW FRIEND

The people in Malindi helped Paula and Stephen move Owen into Paula's truck. Then Paula and Stephen drove back to Haller Park. On the way, they talked about what to do with Owen.

Haller Park already had a few adult hippos. They lived in a fenced-in area, or enclosure (sounds like en-KLO-zhur), with antelopes and other big animals. Owen couldn't live with them. Grown hippos might kick and bite babies they're not related to. The best place for Owen would be with the smaller, gentler animals. They would put him in an enclosure with some monkeys and a few slow-moving tortoises.

At the park, Paula backed the truck up to the enclosure. She and Stephen peeled the nets off Owen. Then they stood back. Owen struggled to his feet. He ran away from the scary people. He ran straight to a giant tortoise and hid behind him. That sure surprised the tortoise!

The tortoise was named Mzee (sounds like mah-ZAY). He was about 130 years old. Owen was about one year old.

Mzee was known for being a bit grumpy. He scooted away from Owen, but Owen stayed close to him. Paula and Stephen left for the night. They never dreamed what they'd see in the morning.

The next day Owen was still peeking out from behind Mzee. But guess what? Mzee wasn't moving away. He even seemed to like the little guy. As for Owen, he saw Mzee was round like a hippo. He was gray like a hippo. Did Owen think Mzee was a hippo? No one knows, but scientists think Mzee's shape and color might have been comforting to Owen.

Hippos in the wild live together in family groups. Owen must have felt very lonely without his hippo family. He was badly in need of a friend.

Over the next few days, it became clear that Mzee was the friend Owen needed. Owen was still very weak. He didn't seem to know what to eat. Stephen added special animal food called dairy cubes to the cabbage, grasses, and carrots he left for Owen and Mzee. When Mzee started to eat a dairy cube, so did Owen. He was copying Mzee!

Owen watched Mzee constantly. He started eating the grasses Mzee ate. He munched the same leaves. It was like Mzee was teaching him what to eat.

In the wild, reptiles like Mzee do not make friends with mammals like Owen. They don't really make friends at all. But over the next few months, Mzee amazed everyone at the sanctuary. The tortoise seemed really fond of the growing hippo.

# Old-Timers

Mzee is an Aldabra (sounds like all-DAH-bruh) tortoise. The Aldabra tortoise is one of the longest-living land animals on Earth.

One of the oldest Aldabra tortoises known to scientists died in 2006. It was 250 years old! That tortoise was alive back when pirates roamed the oceans. Pirates and sailors often kept tortoises and sea turtles on their ships. They weren't pets—they were food. The sailors kept them on their backs so they couldn't run away.

Today, Mzee is about 140 years old. He could live another 100 years or more!

Mzee rested his head on Owen's stomach. He waited for him when they took walks. When they rested, they were always touching each other.

Sometimes Owen nipped at Mzee's back legs. If he wanted his friend to turn left, he'd nip at his left leg. Nip right, turn right. Mzee was happy to go along with this. He gave Owen a few nips of his own. Sometimes if Owen got too slow on a walk, Mzee stretched his neck and nipped Owen's tail. That sure got Owen's attention!

Owen also liked to lick Mzee's head. That was OK. Then he started putting his huge mouth around his Mzee's little head. *That* was a bit much. It made the caretakers pay attention.

Another hippo had hurt Mzee by accident before Owen arrived at the park. That hippo had rolled Mzee like a ball, cracking the top of Mzee's shell. Stephen and Paula called other scientists and vets for advice. They were worried Owen might accidentally hurt Mzee. They were also worried about Owen.

Owen was not acting like a hippo anymore. He was acting like a tortoise! Hippos spend their days in the water. But Owen wanted to be with Mzee. When he should have been napping, he was taking a long, slow walk with Mzee. At night, Owen should have been eating a big dinner. Instead, he ate what Mzee ate.

Paula and Stephen and the other scientists agreed that Owen needed to learn how to be a hippo.

A hippo sniffs a tasty treat. In the wild, hippos can eat more than 80 pounds (35 kg) of grass a day!

# HAPPY HIPPOS

Paula and Stephen decided to build a new enclosure for Owen. They designed one with a waterfall and an island. It had ponds ringed with trees and plants that hippos like to eat. When it was finished, they moved a hippo named Cleo into it first.

Everyone at Haller Park loved Cleo. She liked to balance sticks on her nose. Maybe Cleo and Owen could be friends. Maybe she could teach him to act like a hippo.

Cleo loved the new space. She trotted around it. She swam in every pool.

In December 2006, Stephen and Paula got ready to move Owen into the new space. They piled dairy cubes and bananas at the far side of a sturdy moving box. As they hoped, Owen wandered into the big box to check out the food. They shut the door behind him.

The caretakers lifted the box onto a truck. They drove it to the new enclosure. But before they let Owen out, they moved his pal Mzee to the new space, too. They hoped he would make Owen feel more comfortable in his new home.

When they let Owen out, he ran into

the woods and hid. Mzee went to get him. The two of them walked around the area.

Then Owen heard Cleo. She honked from the pond. Owen was curious but afraid. Smart boy. Cleo was twice his size and more than twice his age. She could do some damage. She was not related to Owen. She might have seen him as a threat.

For the next few days, Cleo chased Owen. Owen ran and hid. Stephen and Paula kept their fingers crossed. They started to think it wasn't going to work. Then one day they found Cleo and Owen in the pond together.

# A Shape to Love

When Owen met Mzee, a man named Peter Greste took a photograph. It was a picture of Owen with his head resting on Mzee's foot. Everyone who saw it fell in love with Owen and Mzee. Dr. Paula helped write a book about the two friends. Lots of kids read the book.

One day, a student in Canada showed her teacher one of the photos in the book. To her, the back of Mzee's shell looked exactly like a hippo face. Maybe that's what Owen saw and liked so much. What do you think?

Cleo popped her head out of the water as Owen dove down head first. Stephen and Paula could see his little tail wagging madly. It made them laugh.

Owen and Cleo started spending more time together. They played a game Stephen called Skipping Hippos. In the pond, Cleo would bounce away from Owen. He bounced after her. When he got close to her, he'd turn and bounce away. Then she bounced back after him. Cleo taught Owen that he could sleep underwater. She also taught him new sounds like honking and bellowing: hippo sounds!

In March 2007, the Haller staff moved Mzee back to his old home. Owen was spending less time with Mzee and more time with Cleo. And Cleo was a little rough with Mzee. Stephen worried about Mzee's safety.

People are sad that Owen and Mzee aren't together anymore. But it's not sad for them. Cleo and Owen are very happy together. Maybe they'll have hippo babies one day. Mzee seems happy, too. There are a few new tortoises in his enclosure. Imagine what Mzee might say if he could tell his new friends about Owen!

THE END

# INDEX

# MORE INFORMATION

To find more information about the animal species in this book and other unusual friendships, check out these books and websites:

*Face to Face With Orangutans*,
by Tim Laman and Cheryl Knott, National Geographic, 2009

*125 True Stories of Amazing Animals*,
National Geographic, 2012

Koko's Kids Club
www.koko.org/kidsclub

San Diego Zoo "Animal Bytes: Hippopotamus"
www.sandiegozoo.org/animalbytes/t-hippopotamus.html

San Francisco Zoo "Animals: Western Lowland Gorilla"
www.sfzoo.org/westernlowlandgorilla

Unlikely Friendships
http://unlikelyfriendshipsbook.tumblr.com

**This book is dedicated to my BFF, Pat Normandeau**
**—A.S.**

# CREDITS

Thanks to National Geographic Channel for the photos of Roscoe and Suryia, as seen on Nat Geo WILD's *Unlikely Animal Friends*.

Inside This Book TOC: Book 1, Best Friends Forever: orangutan and dog, Stevi Calandra/National Geographic Channels; gorilla and kitten, Ron Cohn/Gorilla Foundation/koko.org; dog and fawn, Nuneaton and Warwickshire Wildlife Sanctuary; hippo and tortoise, Associated Press; Title page, Ron Cohn/Gorilla Foundation/koko.org; 4-5, Stevi Calandra/National Geographic Channels; 6, MyrtleBeachSafari.com/Barry Bland; 11 (up, right), Stephaniellen/Shutterstock; 14, MyrtleBeachSafari.com/Barry Bland; 21 (up), Rhett A. Butler/mongabay.com; 22, MyrtleBeachSafari.com/Barry Bland; 26 (up), © Ardiles Rante/Barcroft Media; 28-29, Ron Cohn/Gorilla Foundation/koko.org; 30, Ron Cohn/Gorilla Foundation/koko.org; 34, Ronald Cohn/National Geographic Stock; 36, Ron Cohn/Gorilla Foundation/koko.org; 43, Stuart Key/Dreamstime.com; 44, Ron Cohn/Gorilla Foundation/koko.org; 50, Ron Cohn/Gorilla Foundation/koko.org; 52-53, Caters News Agency; 54, Nuneaton and Warwickshire Wildlife Sanctuary; 61, Utekhina Anna/Shutterstock; 62, Nuneaton and Warwickshire Wildlife Sanctuary; 68, EcoPrint/Shutterstock; 70 (Background), Andrei Calangiu/Dreamstime.com; 70, Nuneaton and Warwickshire Wildlife Sanctuary; 75, Erik Mandre/Dreamstime.com; 76-77, Reuters/Antony Njuguna; 78, Associated Press; 82, Karin Van Ijzendoorn/Dreamstime.com; 86, Associated Press; 91, Daniel Wilson/Shutterstock; 94, Rgbe/Dreamstime.com; 98, Reuters/Antony Njuguna; 102, MyrtleBeachSafari.com/Barry Bland.

# ACKNOWLEDGMENTS

Amy Shields thanks the following organizations for helping make this book possible:

The Gorilla Foundation
www.koko.org

Nuneaton & Warwickshire Wildlife Sanctuary
www.nuneatonwildlife.co.uk

Owen & Mzee
www.owenandmzee.com

T.I.G.E.R.S.
www.suryiaandroscoe.com

# THE WHALE WHO WON HEARTS!

## And More True Stories of Adventures With Animals

Brian Skerry With
Kathleen Weidner Zoehfeld

**Published by the National Geographic Society**

John M. Fahey, *Chairman of the Board and Chief Executive Officer*
Declan Moore, *Executive Vice President; President, Publishing and Travel*
Melina Gerosa Bellows, *Publisher and Chief Creative Officer, Books, Kids, and Family*

**Prepared by the Book Division**
Hector Sierra, *Senior Vice President and General Manager*
Nancy Laties Feresten, *Senior Vice President, Kids Publishing and Media*
Jennifer Emmett, *Vice President, Editorial Director, Kids Books*
Eva Absher-Schantz, *Design Director, Kids Publishing and Media*
Jay Sumner, *Director of Photography, Kids Publishing*
R. Gary Colbert, *Production Director*
Jennifer A. Thornton, *Director of Managing Editorial*

**Staff for This Book**
Becky Baines, Shelby Alinsky, *Project Editors*
Marfé Ferguson Delano, *Editor*
Kelley Miller, *Senior Photo Editor*
Amanda Larsen, *Art Director*
Ruth Ann Thompson, *Designer*
Ariane Szu-Tu, *Editorial Assistant*
Callie Broaddus, *Design Production Assistant*
Margaret Leist, *Illustrations Assistant*
Grace Hill, *Associate Managing Editor*
Joan Gossett, *Production Editor*
Lewis R. Bassford, *Production Manager*
Susan Borke, *Legal and Business Affairs*

**Production Services**
Phillip L. Schlosser, *Senior Vice President*
Chris Brown, *Vice President, NG Book Manufacturing*
George Bounelis, *Senior Production Manager*
Nicole Elliott, *Director of Production*
Rachel Faulise, *Manager*
Robert L. Barr, *Manager*

The National Geographic Society is one of the world's largest nonprofit scientific and educational organizations. Founded in 1888 to "increase and diffuse geographic knowledge," the Society's mission is to inspire people to care about the planet. It reaches more than 400 million people worldwide each month through its official journal, *National Geographic*, and other magazines; National Geographic Channel; television documentaries; music; radio; films; books; DVDs; maps; exhibitions; live events; school publishing programs; interactive media; and merchandise. National Geographic has funded more than 10,000 scientific research, conservation, and exploration projects and supports an education program promoting geographic literacy.

For more information, please visit www.nationalgeographic.com, call 1-800-NGS LINE (647-5463), or write to the following address:

National Geographic Society, 1145 17th Street N.W., Washington, D.C. 20036-4688 U.S.A.

Visit us online at www.nationalgeographic.com/books

For librarians and teachers: www.ngchildrensbooks.org

National Geographic supports K–12 educators with ELA Common Core Resources. Visit natgeoed.org/commoncore for more information.

More for kids from National Geographic: kids.nationalgeographic.com

For information about special discounts for bulk purchases, please contact National Geographic Books Special Sales: ngspecsales@ngs.org

For rights or permissions inquiries, please contact National Geographic Books Subsidiary Rights: ngbookrights@ngs.org

Trade paperback ISBN:
978-1-4263-1520-6
Reinforced library edition ISBN:
978-1-4263-1521-3

# Table of CONTENTS

Five female leatherback sea turtles scoot up onto the beach to lay their eggs.

# Quest for LIVING DINOSAURS

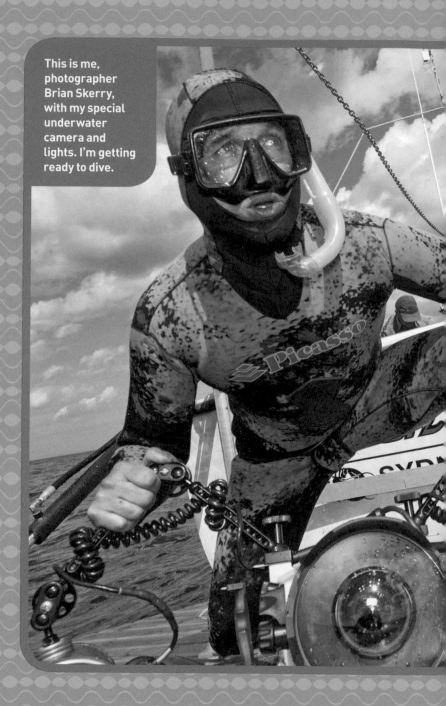

This is me, photographer Brian Skerry, with my special underwater camera and lights. I'm getting ready to dive.

## Chapter 1

# A SHOT in the DARK

It was a warm night in May. I was walking along a beach in Trinidad (sounds like TRIH-nuh-dad), an island in the Caribbean (sounds like CARE-uh-BEE-un) Sea. It was almost midnight. The ocean waves rumbled and crashed onto the sand. Behind the beach, palm trees swayed in the damp breeze.

Suddenly, a few yards down, I spotted dark shapes on the sand.

They looked like huge rocks. But they were leatherback sea turtles! They were here to do something sea turtles have been doing for more than 100 million years. And I was hoping to shoot them. With my camera, that is!

My name is Brian Skerry. I'm an underwater wildlife photographer. It's my job to take pictures of animals that live in the sea.

I fell in love with the sea when I was a child. I grew up in a small town in Massachusetts. We lived about an hour's drive from the ocean. I was always asking my parents to take me there.

When I wasn't at the beach, I was

reading books or watching TV shows about ocean life. I really admired the sea turtles. It was fun to imagine gliding with them through miles of deep, blue water.

When I was 15, I tried scuba diving. It was in my family's swimming pool. I was sitting in the shallow end. I had the scuba tank on my back. Hoses attached to the tank would bring air to my mouthpiece. I'll never forget putting that mouthpiece in and taking my first breath underwater. All I could think was, "Wow! I have discovered a whole new world!"

As I grew up, I practiced diving. I studied photography in college. I began taking underwater photos. Finally, I landed my dream job. I was hired to take photos for *National Geographic* magazine.

And that's what brought me to Trinidad. I was there to photograph sea turtles for National Geographic.

Sea turtles are reptiles. Like all reptiles, they breathe air. But unlike most reptiles, sea turtles don't live on land. They spend nearly their entire lives in the ocean. That's why they're called marine reptiles.

One hundred million years ago, dinosaurs ruled the land. At that time, many types of marine reptiles lived in the oceans. Giant, long-necked plesiosaurs (sounds like PLEEZ-ee-oh-soars) and sharp-toothed ichthyosaurs (sounds like ICK-thee-oh-soars) swam the seas. Earth's first sea turtles swam with them.

Dinosaurs died out 65 million years ago. Marine reptiles went extinct then, too—all of them except for sea turtles, that is.

Seven types of sea turtles are still around today. The leatherback is the largest of them all. Leatherbacks can grow to more than seven feet (2 m) long. They can weigh more than 2,000 pounds (900 kg).

Other types of sea turtles have hard shells. Not leatherback sea turtles. They have thick, leathery skin. It's what gives them their name.

My assistant Mauricio (sounds like moh-REE-cee-oh) Handler was with me on the beach. As we watched, the giant female leatherbacks began to dig their nests and lay their eggs. Female leatherbacks always lay their eggs on warm, sandy beaches. Usually they return to the same beach where they were born.

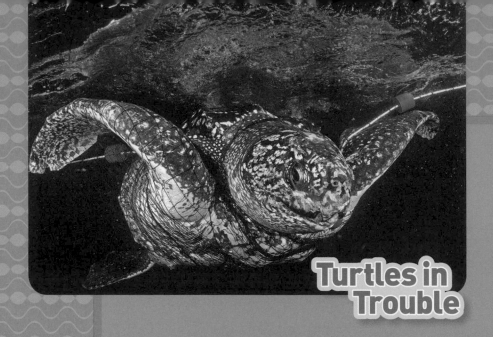

# Turtles in Trouble

Sadly, leatherback turtles are in danger of extinction. People have been hunting leatherbacks for centuries. But over the past 30 years, too many have been killed for their meat. People raided nests and took all the eggs. Today, new laws help protect nesting leatherbacks and their eggs. But they still face many dangers. They get tangled in fishnets. They get hooked on longlines meant to catch large fish. Houses and hotels have also been built on some of the leatherbacks' favorite nesting beaches.

I moved in close to one of the turtles. Leatherbacks only come out when it is dark. I knew the camera flashbulb would disturb her. So I would rely on the moonlight.

The turtle found a spot she liked. She made a shallow pit in the sand with her front flippers. Once she was comfy, she dug a deep hole with her hind flippers. She took long, deep breaths as she dug. To me, it was like a sound from the prehistoric (sounds like pre-hih-STORE-ick) past! She laid more than 80 round, white eggs in the hole. Then she covered them with sand.

We watched as the turtle headed back to the water. Having a chance to photograph this huge creature in the wild was thrilling—almost like seeing a living dinosaur!

A newly hatched baby leatherback scurries to the sea. It will spend the rest of its life in the water.

## Chapter 2

# TRAPPED in a Net!

It takes 60 to 70 days for a leatherback's babies to come out of their eggs. While we were taking photos of the nesting leatherbacks, eggs from other nests began to hatch. We stopped to take photos as the tiny, striped hatchlings hurried across the sand. Their mothers were long gone. Leatherback babies must look to the sea for food and protection.

For the lucky few who make it to adulthood, there aren't many ocean creatures that can harm them. But humans have created new problems for these ancient (sounds like ANE-chunt) animals. I wanted to see for myself the dangers leatherbacks face once they leave the shore. It was time to get into the water!

I talked to local fishermen and found one who was interested in helping. He said leatherbacks sometimes got tangled in his fishnets. He did what he could to save them. But sometimes he was too late. If a tangled turtle is not pulled to the surface soon enough, it will drown.

The fisherman said we could follow him while he fished. If any turtles got caught, we could see how it happened. Maybe we could even help. We rented a small boat. The captain of our boat helped us sail close behind the fishing boat.

We watched as the fisherman set out a mile (1.6 km) of fishnet. Floats held up the top edge of the net. The rest of it hung down in the water, like a curtain. After several hours, the fisherman pulled in his net. Dozens of fish were caught in it. He put the fish in his boat. Then he set the net out again.

Our captain moved our boat slowly alongside the net. I sat in the front of the boat. The stars shone brightly above us. I kept an eye on the net below. I had my fins, mask, and air tank ready, in case I needed to dive.

Later that night, Mauricio and I spotted an adult turtle in the net. I quickly pulled on my diving gear and went over the side. As I swam down, I could see the leatherback struggling.

Leatherbacks never stop swimming. The turtle paddled and paddled with its long flippers. The more it paddled, the more tangled it became. I took a few pictures of it. Then I had to help it. I grabbed my knife and began to cut the net.

As I worked, the current began to wrap me up in the net, too. I had to stop helping the turtle and cut myself free first. Then I cut the turtle loose. I watched as it swam off gracefully, into the darkness of the sea.

# Chowing Down

Jellyfish, or jellies, are a leatherback's favorite food. Jellies are mostly water, with a few minerals and a dash of protein thrown in. How do leatherbacks grow so big on a jelly diet? The answer: they eat a LOT of jellies. Scientists videotaped one leatherback eating 69 jellies in three hours. Each jelly weighed about ten pounds (4.5 kg). That's 690 pounds (313 kg) of jellies! A leatherback's throat is lined with three-inch (7.6-cm) spines. These spines help the turtle swallow its very slippery prey—and keep the prey from coming back up.

I found this leatherback swimming in deep water. The two yellow fish clinging to her side are called remoras.

## Chapter 3

# Into the WILD!

**N**ow I had pictures of a leatherback underwater. But I wanted to take photos of one swimming. I knew I'd find turtles swimming around Trinidad. But the water there is too murky to get good photos. I needed to find leatherbacks in clear water. So I went to the other side of the world. To the Pacific Ocean!

I headed for one of the turtles'

favorite hunting grounds. It is in the deep water off the Kai (sounds like KEY) Islands in Indonesia (sounds like in-doh-NEE-zhuh).

My assistant Jeff Wildermuth joined me on this trip. When we got to the Kai Islands, we talked to some local fishermen. They gave us tips on how to find turtles.

The fishermen go out to sea in long, narrow boats. Boats like this have been used in these islands for thousands of years. I decided to use one of them to search for leatherbacks. I knew it could be dangerous. The boats are very tippy when the waves get steep! But this was my best bet for getting close to the turtles.

The local people told us they often found turtles around a certain island.

Jeff and I set up our tents on the beach there. Then we decided to try our luck.

Jeff and I eased our boat off the sand and into the choppy water. We watched for the glint of a black turtle moving under the silvery waves. Meanwhile, the sun blazed down on us. We gulped water from our water bottles. We paddled around the whole island, searching. Before we knew it, the sun was going down. We hadn't seen one turtle.

Back at camp, we checked to make sure there were no scorpions under our sleeping bags. We pulled our mosquito nets around us. Then we fell fast asleep.

The next morning, we went off in our boat again. Hour after hour, we watched and waited for leatherbacks. No luck.

## What You Can Do

Here are some ways you can help sea turtles continue to survive:

- Make less trash, and pick up trash at the beach. Plastic bags can end up being washed into the sea. Many leatherbacks are killed when they eat plastic bags. To them, the bags look like jellyfish.

- Stay away from sea turtle nesting areas. If you live near a nesting beach, keep your lights low during nesting season.

- Design a poster. Write a report. Give a talk. Help people understand how important Earth's oceans are!

Scientists have learned that it takes 20 to 30 years for a female leatherback to grow old enough to lay eggs. But over the last 30 years, people have been stealing the eggs from leatherback nests. It's clear that this has hurt the turtles. It has left very few young ones to grow up in the sea.

Day after day, Jeff and I waited and watched. We felt sad that this vast ocean is now nearly empty of leatherbacks.

On the fourth day, we spotted our first turtle! I grabbed my camera and slipped quickly into the water. I didn't put on any of my diving gear, except for my fins. Leatherbacks are fast swimmers, and I thought the gear would slow me down. Still, I couldn't keep up. The leatherback was gone in a flash.

In three weeks, we saw leatherbacks only three times. I tried to take some good photos. But I had no luck.

Finally, near the end of our stay, we spotted a beautiful female. She was coming up for a breath. And she was moving pretty slowly. I slipped into the water and swam alongside her. She saw me and began to dive.

She made slow, steady strokes with her flippers. She moved through the water easily, like a bird flying through the air. I swam as hard as I could to keep up. Fishy tagalongs called remoras (sounds like reh-MORE-ahs) clung to her sides. A school of little fish swam out in front of her.

Nearly out of breath, I managed to get a few shots. I hoped they would be good ones! Exhausted, I stopped kicking. Then I drifted to the surface. Jeff and I watched as the turtle faded into the blue.

That night, I checked my shots. We had searched the sea for weeks. Some days, we didn't think we'd survive the brutal sun and biting bugs. But yes! We had finally gotten a good photo of a leatherback in the wild. It's the one on page 20 of this book.

The giant turtle looked like a living starship traveling through her underwater universe. We could only hope that our work would help people understand what these awesome animals are going through.

> **Did You Know?**
>
> **Leatherbacks swim longer distances than any other turtle. They've been tracked traveling more than 6,500 miles (10,460 km).**

Surrounded by
sea ice, a mother
harp seal and
I take a look at
each other.

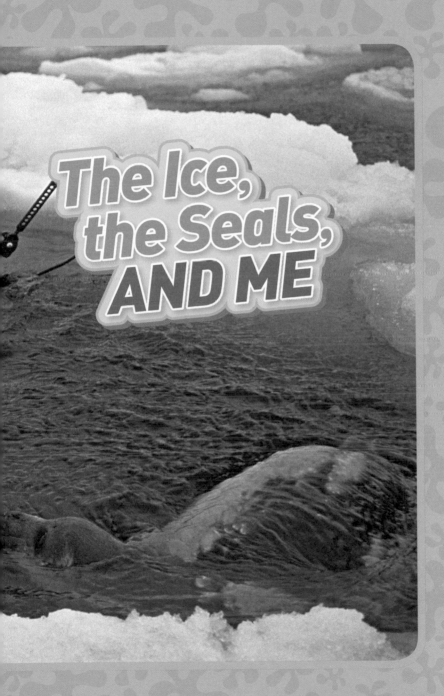

# The Ice,
# the Seals,
# AND ME

A white harp seal pup is safe on the ice. The pup's mom looks on from the water.

# Chapter 1

# The Whitecoats ARRIVE

**H**arp seals live in the icy waters of the North Atlantic and Arctic Oceans. But every year in early spring, thousands of them swim south to Canada's Gulf of St. Lawrence. The females gather in small groups on top of the sea ice. That's where they give birth to their pups.

Most photographers use helicopters to reach the seals.

Harp seals get their name from the harp-shaped band of dark fur found on the backs of adults.

That way they can stay on the ice for a few hours and then fly home. I wanted more than a few hours with the seals. I wanted to take photos of them at all different times of day.

In early spring I flew to the Magdalen (sounds like MAG-duh-lin) Islands, a group of small islands in the gulf. Fishing is a way of life for the people here. At this time of year, the sea ice begins to break up. The fishermen get ready to sail. They will stay out in the gulf for many days at a time. That's exactly what I wanted to do!

Some local fishermen agreed to take me out with them. The captain and his two-man crew welcomed me and my assistant

Sean (sounds like SHAWN) Whelan aboard. Their 65-foot (20-m) boat would be our home for the next 17 days.

I stared out at the frozen sea. I couldn't imagine how we were going to get anywhere. Thick sheets of ice still covered the water. There were just a few cracks here and there. The captain told me not to worry. He knew how to move the boat through the narrow openings. Plus, this was no ordinary fishing boat! It was built tough. The body, or hull, of the boat was made of thick steel.

Not long after we left the dock, our ship's strength was tested. We found ourselves iced in. We were completely surrounded by ice. But the captain knew how to break out. He powered the boat up on top of the ice. We could hear the steel hull crunching the ice below. Once we'd made a new crack, we sailed on a little farther. Then we hit solid ice again. And again the captain powered the ship through.

After several hours of this, we spotted a group of harp seals on the ice up ahead. I watched them for a while, from the deck. It looked like they would soon give birth to their pups. I couldn't wait to get out on the ice with them!

We stayed near the seals for many days. Each morning I woke up at six and put on my thermal underwear, socks, fleece sweater, ski goggles, parka, and warm boots. I grabbed my cameras. Then I walked quietly out onto the ice.

# Sleek Swimmers

Harp seals are swift hunters. They dive as deep as 1,000 feet (305 meters) in search of fish, shrimp, and crabs to eat. They can stay underwater for as long as 15 minutes. But like all mammals, they must come up to the surface to breathe. There are three different groups of harp seals in the Arctic. In the spring, each group returns to its favorite breeding area, either in the Gulf of St. Lawrence, the Greenland Sea, or the White Sea. Adult harp seals grow to be five to six feet (1.5 to 1.8 m) long. They can weigh up to 400 pounds (180 kg).

On my very first day, a few pups were born. Newborn harp seals are light yellow. In just a day or two, they turn snowy white. The young pups are called "whitecoats." Their fluffy fur protects them from the freezing air. But it doesn't keep them warm in the icy cold water. If they fall in, they will quickly get too cold and drown.

Each pup stayed close to the spot where it was born. Like most babies, they spent a lot of time sleeping. On sunny days, the ice melted under them, creating seal-shaped cradles in the ice.

After giving birth, the mother seals spent much of their time in the water. But they were never far from their babies. When a pup was hungry it cried, *Mmaaaa! Mmaaaa!* Then up popped its mother through a crack in the ice. She sniffed the pup, just to be sure it was hers. Then she flopped on her side and let the pup nurse.

I was amazed at how quickly the pups grew. Seal milk has ten times the fat of cow's milk. Pups gain five pounds (2.3 kg) a day on their moms' milk. By the time they're ten days old, they weigh more than 70 pounds (32 kg). Mother harp seals only nurse their pups for 12 days. Then they swim off for good, leaving the pups on their own. These pups have to grow fast!

By midmorning each day, I headed back to the ship. I ate a hearty breakfast of eggs, bacon, and sausages, and plenty of hot coffee. Then it was time to dive.

Here I am, under the sea ice with my camera and lights. A special diving suit helps protect me from the supercold seawater.

**DEADLY ICE**

Cold water can be deadly if a diver's not prepared. And here the seawater is supercold! It's even colder than the temperature at which ice cubes freeze solid. In subfreezing temperatures like this, an unprotected human can only survive a few moments.

First, I pulled on layers of thermal underwear. Then I put

on my dry suit. Unlike a wet suit, which divers use in warm water, a dry suit keeps water out. Mine has boots and gloves attached. Next, I pulled on two separate hoods. The first one, called an "ice hood," covers my head and face. It has holes for my eyes and mouth. The second hood is open for my face, but it protects my head and neck.

Last, I put on my mask and settled my air tank on my back. Then I slipped through a hole in the ice. The ice above my head looked like an upside-down mountain range. Icy peaks and valleys rolled on as far as I could see. Sunbeams sparkled through gaps in the ice. It was a crystal kingdom of emerald green that glowed from above.

The mother seals glided gracefully through the water. They were shy about getting too close to me. So I hid behind a ledge of ice, just below one of their breathing holes. I waited for good shots to come along. And I waited. Often, the main skill a wildlife photographer needs is patience.

While they were nursing their pups, the moms hardly had any chance to eat. After 12 days, they were getting very hungry! One by one, they began to swim away. They headed north to feed.

The pups now had a thick layer of fat, called blubber, under their skin. At the same time, they were beginning to shed their white fur.

## Did You Know?

Adult harp seals can swim more than 2,500 miles (4,023 km) from their hunting grounds to their breeding grounds.

Underneath was a smooth, speckled gray coat. This new fur, along with their fat, would help keep them warm in the icy water.

Left all alone on the ice, the spotted gray pups cried for their moms. But no moms returned. The pups began to slide into the icy sea for a few minutes at a time. Then they crawled back up onto the ice. At this stage, they're called "beaters," because of the awkward way they beat the water with their flippers.

The pups were easier to photograph underwater than the adults. They were still beginning swimmers. But each day they swam a little longer and dove a little deeper. They were figuring out the watery world that would soon be their home.

One evening, as twilight settled in,

I took a few more photos on the ice. Then I climbed aboard the boat for the night. I listened to the pups, still calling for their moms in the darkness. I felt good about our work so far. But trouble can arrive quickly on the ice.

At two o'clock in the morning, one of the fishermen shook me awake. "The captain wants to see you," he said. I climbed the ladder to the ship's control room. I found the captain staring out at a swirling world of white. There was a blizzard raging outside.

"The ice is against the hull now," he said. "We'll be crushed sometime soon and will sink."

This was a tough boat. But now hurricane-force winds were slamming giant slabs of sea ice against us. Few boats can withstand that. The captain radioed for help. But we were far from the islands. It could take a long time for help to arrive.

The captain ordered us to get into our survival suits. In warm places, a good life jacket may be enough to help you survive a shipwreck. Near the Arctic, you need a thick, head-to-toe suit that will help you float and keep you warm.

For two hours, Sean and I sat on deck with the crew. We listened to the wind howl. We waited for the groaning sound of buckling, or crumpling, steel. In the glow of the ship's spotlight, we stared at the huge slabs of ice surrounding us. The idea that we might have to jump off the boat and onto that ice was truly terrifying.

# Harp Seal Talk

Harp seals have good hearing, especially underwater. When a mother seal is underwater, she can hear her pup when it cries for her up on the ice. When pups play together on the ice, they make cute mumbling sounds. Adults call to each other, too. Big male seals growl and warble at each other. This can mean "back off!" Adults are really chatty when they're looking for mates. Scientists have counted more than 19 different sounds harp seals make underwater. These include chirps, trills, and clicks.

This whitecoat looked right at me with its big, dark eyes. The pup's fluffy fur protects it from freezing air.

# Chapter 3

# SINK or SWIM!

Lucky for us, the steel did not buckle. And sometime after four o'clock, we were rescued! A huge Canadian Coast Guard ship arrived. It cut a path through the ice. We followed it. Nine hours later, we made it back to the Magdalen Islands.

For us, the blizzard was a brush with disaster. But it was just an extra-exciting night on the ice for the harp seals. They are at home here.

I knew the pups I had photographed would soon be swimming north. As long as they're on the ice, seals are easy targets for hungry polar bears. Still, it's safer for them in the gulf than it is up north. That's why the moms come here to give birth. Fewer polar bears stalk the ice here.

**Did You Know?**

**A mother harp seal can pick out her baby from hundreds of others by its smell.**

Once the pups are ready to swim north, they will stay in the water most of their lives. Then, sharks and orcas, or killer whales, will become a big danger. It's safer for pups to practice swimming in the gulf. They can become fast swimmers before having to face their natural enemies.

In the gulf, humans are the pups' biggest threat. They have long hunted harp seals for their oil, fur, and skin. In the 1940s, the white coats of the newborn pups became popular. Hundreds of thousands of pups were killed to make fur coats.

In 1987, it became against the law to hunt and kill the "whitecoat" pups. But by then, harp seals were in danger of extinction. Today, humans still hunt harp seals. But there are limits on how many seals hunters can take.

Harp seals are slowly making a comeback. But the danger is far from over. In recent years, thick sea ice has begun to melt. It is starting to vanish from the gulf. If that ice goes, the seals may no longer have any safe places to give birth.

# Vanishing Ice

All over the globe, the climate is changing. As people burn fossil fuels, such as oil and coal, carbon dioxide (sounds like die-OX-ide) is released into the atmosphere (sounds like AT-muhs-fear). Carbon dioxide is a greenhouse gas. It causes Earth's atmosphere to trap the sun's warmth, much the way the glass in a greenhouse does. As the amount of carbon dioxide increases, more and more of the sun's heat is trapped. This is causing Earth's average temperature to rise. And as the Earth gets warmer, more sea ice melts.

During my time in the gulf, I saw many pups die because they fell into the water before they were ready. In the future, harp seals may have to have their pups farther north. The ice may be more solid up there. But there are also more killer whales and polar bears.

The more I saw of harp seals, the more I admired them. Even after our scary night on the boat, I looked forward to getting out on the ice with them again. This time I went out in a helicopter! My hands and feet ached and went numb with the cold. I had to wear ski goggles to shield my eyes from the biting wind and snow. But the thrill of seeing these creatures in their beautiful frozen world made it all worth it!

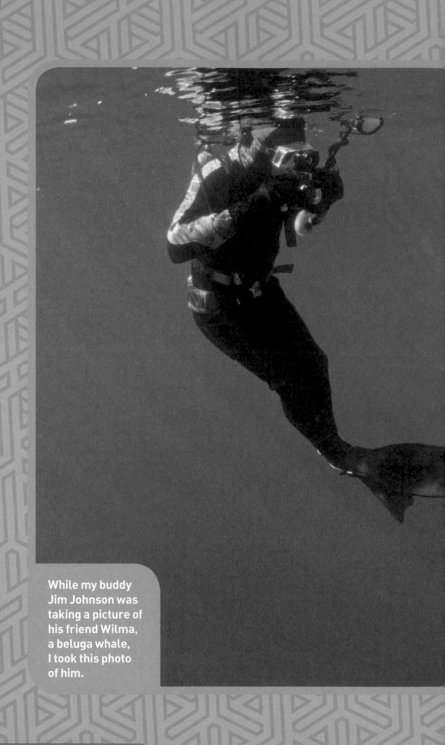

While my buddy Jim Johnson was taking a picture of his friend Wilma, a beluga whale, I took this photo of him.

# THE WHALE
# Who Won
# HEARTS

People in a canoe come out to meet Wilma as she swims with a diver.

## Chapter 1

**A NEW Friend!**

When I was a kid, I loved learning about whales. I sometimes even dreamed about having a whale as my best friend. I'd put on my mask, snorkel, and fins. Then I'd swim back and forth in my backyard swimming pool. All the time I'd be imagining that I was deep under the ocean waves, with a whale as my guide. What a magical experience it would be, to explore the ocean with a whale as a friend!

Of course, whales are wild animals. They hunt and swim together in small groups called pods. They don't usually make friends with humans.

Now that I'm an underwater photographer, I sometimes get asked to take photos of whales. To get those photos, I go out into the ocean and search for the whales. I never thought a whale might come find me! But that's just what happened to an old diving buddy of mine.

His name is Jim Johnson. Jim lives in Nova Scotia (sounds like NO-vah SKO-shah), in Canada. One day, Jim called me and said that the most amazing thing had happened. A young female beluga whale had come into the bay near his home. And, he said, he had become good friends with her. I could hardly believe it! Jim told me to come on up and meet her.

When I got there, Jim told me the whole story. A few months earlier, some local fishermen had spotted a beluga whale in Chedabucto (sounds like shed-ah-BOUK-toe) Bay. Belugas normally live in the ice-cold waters of the Arctic Ocean. The fishermen knew it was unusual to see a beluga as far south as Nova Scotia. They figured she was just passing through. But a few days later, they saw her again. They told their families and friends about the lonely white whale in the bay.

Chedabucto Bay is a peaceful place. Green, wooded hills line its shores.

Eagles soar in the sky above. Fishing boats rock gently in the quiet harbor. No one knew why the beluga stopped there. Maybe it felt like a welcoming place. Before long, people all around the bay began talking about her. *Why was she still here?* they wondered. She looked young. Maybe she was lost and alone.

The young whale seemed to like the red buoy (sounds like BOO-ee) that bobbed in the middle of the bay. Buoys are floating signs that are anchored in place. They help fishermen and other boaters find their way. Very often, when fishermen passed this buoy, they would see the whale. The buoy's rusty anchor chain rattled and clinked as it rocked in the waves. The buoy's small bell clanged.

# Meet the Beluga

Beluga whales are often called white whales. They are among the world's smallest whales. Adults can measure up to 20 feet (6 m) long. Males can weigh up to 3,000 pounds (1,360 kg). Belugas hunt for fish, squid, and shrimp. They also eat crabs and marine worms. Beluga whales can dive as deep as 3,300 feet (1,000 m). They can stay underwater for as long as 25 minutes. But they must come up to the surface to breathe. Like most whales, a beluga breathes air through a blowhole on top of its head.

Whales sing and call to one another across great distances underwater. Beluga whales are very chatty. They are constantly making all kinds of sounds. They chirp and squeak. They clang and whistle. Maybe the young whale felt comforted by the buoy's constant clinking and clanging.

It didn't take long for Jim to hear about the white whale. He's lived on the shore of Chedabucto Bay all his life. He has traveled around the world in great sailing ships. He has lived among seals in the frozen north. He has searched for treasure off the sandy shores of tropical islands. He has been face to face with all kinds of ocean life. But, just like me, one thing he had always dreamed of was swimming with a whale. Jim was thrilled to learn a young beluga was right in his own "backyard." He couldn't wait to meet her.

Jim got his diving gear ready. He loaded it onto his small, inflatable boat. Then he motored his little boat across the water to a small, rocky beach. From here he could see the red buoy. He pulled his boat up on the beach. He put on his diving gear and slipped into the water. He swam down about 20 feet (6 m). He wasn't sure what to expect. He hoped to see the white whale. But he didn't think she'd come very close to him.

**Did You Know?**

Newborn belugas are dark gray. Over the next five years, they grow lighter and lighter in color.

Wilma loved to have her picture taken! Here she is by the red buoy.

# A WHALE Named WILMA

Jim stared out into the green water. He could see some seashells on the bottom. A few small fish swam past. For what seemed like ages, that is all he saw. He knelt on the bottom. He shivered. He didn't think he could stay under much longer. Then, from out of nowhere, the whale appeared!

She swam slowly toward him at first. Then she moved away,

disappearing into the murky water like a ghost. But she soon came back. She circled around him. And then she stopped right in front of him. Jim stayed very still. His heart pounded. This was no ghost! Right before his eyes, just inches away, was a wild beluga whale.

Very slowly, Jim stretched out his hand. The whale stared at him. Jim wanted to pet her, but he didn't want to frighten her. He waited. She moved toward him. Then, very gently, she pushed the top of her head against his palm. Jim rubbed her head. He ran his hand down her side. She let him stroke her back. Then, as quickly as she had appeared, she swam away into the sea.

A wild whale! He had reached out and petted a wild whale!

As the weeks went by, people continued to spot the young beluga in the bay. They began to think of her as a member of their community. Someone began calling her Wilma, and the name stuck.

Every day, Jim put on his diving gear and swam out to meet Wilma. Much to his surprise, Wilma seemed to like his company. Their friendship grew quickly.

But it was not always easy to find Wilma in the murky water. Jim had to think of a way to let her know when he was there.

## Did You Know?

**Beluga whales make so many different kinds of high-pitched chirps and twitters, they are often called "sea canaries."**

He knew that whales in the wild call to each other to stay in touch. They also make clicking sounds that help them find their way. When the clicks hit an object such as a fish or rock, the sounds bounce back as echoes. By listening to the echoes, belugas can figure out where and what something is. This is called echolocation (sounds like EH-ko-lo-KAY-shun).

Jim wondered if he could create a call that would get Wilma's attention. Then, using echolocation, maybe she could find him in the water. He got an idea. He picked up two stones and banged them together underwater. It worked like a charm! A few minutes later, up swam Wilma. She knew exactly where he was. From then on, Jim used this signal to let Wilma know he had come to visit. Within ten minutes, he would spot the whale swimming his way.

# Melon Head

The beluga's forehead is very unusual. It is big and rounded. It feels like a balloon filled with warm butter. That "balloon" is called the melon. It is actually a fatty lens. The lenses in a pair of eyeglasses focus light. The beluga's melon focuses sound. It focuses the clicks belugas make when they are echolocating. A beluga can change the shape of its melon whenever it needs to. This lets it point its clicks in different directions and focus the clicks at different distances.

Wilma swims below a boy floating with a life jacket. The beluga even rubs her back against his foot.

## Chapter 3

# A DREAM COME TRUE

I was blown away by Jim's story! I couldn't wait to get some photos of him with his new friend.

The next morning after breakfast, Jim took me to meet Wilma. We got into our diving gear and slipped into the water. Jim banged two rocks together, and Wilma soon appeared. It thrilled me to meet her! Together, she and I searched the seafloor for treasures.

We found sand dollars and clam shells. Wilma seemed curious about everything.

Every now and then, she would turn upside down and rub her head on the bottom. That's a good way to scratch your head, when you don't have hands!

Taking photos of Wilma was so much fun. She loved to ham it up for the camera. Later in the morning, she started a game of catch with a piece of kelp, a type of seaweed. She plucked a frond of kelp from the bottom. Then she swam up to the surface with it and let it go. As the kelp drifted down, Wilma dove under it and caught it on her head. Then she swam

**Did You Know?**

Beluga whales can live as long as 35 to 50 years in the wild.

back up and started the game all over again.

Jim and I laughed at her silly game. He told me that once he accidentally dropped his car keys over the side of the boat. He groaned as he watched them sink into the water. Without much hope, he put on his diving gear and got ready to go looking for them. But before he even got into the water, Wilma popped up with the keys in her mouth. What a great friend!

After a long morning of playing and exploring, Wilma took a rest near the red buoy. Jim floated quietly nearby, and Wilma moved in close. She looked like a big puppy getting ready to snuggle up on the couch. She loved having the top of her head scratched. As Jim petted her, her eyes closed. She seemed to go into a trance.

# A Whale of a Challenge

When the Arctic Ocean freezes in winter, beluga whales swim south to warmer waters. If they wait too long to leave, they can get trapped by the Arctic ice. Then they will be easy targets for hungry polar bears and orcas. But human hunters are the belugas' biggest threat. Over the years, overfishing has nearly wiped out some populations. Today, laws limit the fishing of belugas. In some areas, however, beluga whales are still in danger of going extinct.

When we climbed back into the boat to head home, Wilma rubbed along the boat's smooth sides. Jim reached down to say goodbye, and the beluga took his hand gently into her mouth.

Jim told me that he sometimes saw Wilma playing with pilot whales. Sometimes she swam with seals, or with the local divers who gathered sea urchins. People came in boats, canoes, and kayaks to meet her. Of all her visitors, Wilma seemed to love children the most. She let them touch her head and stroke her sides. But Wilma never had the company of her own kind. Jim knew that Wilma was lonely.

Exploring the sea with Wilma was my dream come true. I wanted to stay with her forever. But I had to go home. I was sad to leave Wilma. But I was happy that she had Jim as a friend.

Wilma lived in the bay for many more years. Then one day, I got a call from Jim. Earlier that spring, he had put on his diving gear and gone out to look for Wilma as usual. He peered through the water, but he couldn't find her. He picked up two stones and banged them together. This time, his signal did not work.

Jim got back into his boat. He sailed all around the bay. He returned the next day, and the day after that. Wilma was nowhere to be found. Over the next few months, Jim checked the bay from time to time. But in his heart, he knew that Wilma was gone.

I knew how sad Jim felt. We talked about his special friendship with Wilma. Although he would always miss her, maybe this was for the best. She was a wild animal, free to roam the sea. She needed to find other beluga whales. Maybe she would even start a family. Wilma had come into the bay on her own. She had left on her own. And that's the way it should be.

Jim and I like to imagine that Wilma is out there in the wide sea, having adventures with other whales. We wonder if she's telling them the story of her life among humans. We hope one day we'll see her again. As long as we live, none of us who met Wilma will ever forget this magical gift from the sea.

Gray reef sharks swim over the corals around the Line Islands in the Pacific Ocean.

# THE REEF
## Where
## SHARKS RULE

I took this photo of a diver feeding a shark a fish. He used special gloves to protect his hands from accidental bites.

## Chapter 1

# HOOKED ON SHARKS

'll never forget the first time I swam with a shark. It was almost 30 years ago. At that time, most people thought of sharks as sharp-toothed killing machines. The last thing any diver wanted was to run into a shark! But I had a chance to help a group of scientists. They were studying sharks off the coast of Rhode Island. Even though I was a little afraid, I joined them.

I thought it would be interesting to get to know these animals better.

We sailed 20 miles (32 km) offshore. The scientists put out some bait. A five-foot (1.5-m)-long blue shark swam up to check it out. I was in the water taking photos. For more than an hour, I drifted in the chilly water. The shark swam right beside me. But it never tried to attack. It just seemed curious. And I was curious about the shark. All my fears melted away. I stared at it in total awe. The shark had a slender body. It had long, winglike fins. It looked like a finely designed aircraft.

Ever since that day, I've been hooked on sharks. I've swum with blue sharks many times since then. I've swum with other kinds, too. Thanks to scientists and explorers, people have begun to better understand sharks. They're no longer seen as monsters. Like lions in the grasslands of Africa, sharks are the top predators in their ocean homes. Predators are animals that hunt other animals for food. But sharks never hunt humans on purpose.

It can be scary to hear about a shark biting a surfer at the beach. But such attacks are very, very rare. A shark may strike if a human threatens it. Or it may mistake a human for a seal or other natural prey. But humans are a greater danger to sharks than they are to us.

## Did You Know?

Whenever a shark loses a tooth, a new one comes in to replace it. A shark can grow thousands of teeth in its lifetime.

# The Scoop on Sharks

Sharks first swam the seas around 400 million years ago. That's almost 200 million years before the first dinosaur walked on Earth. A shark's skeleton is not bony. It's made up mostly of cartilage (sounds like CAR-tuh-lij). Your ears and the tip of your nose are also made of cartilage. Today, there are more than 400 types of shark. The smallest is the dwarf lantern shark. It's smaller than a human hand. The biggest shark is the whale shark (above). It's as long as a school bus!

People kill more than 100 million sharks each year. Most are taken for their fins, which are used in shark fin soup.

Way too often, I see badly hurt sharks. I see some tangled in long fish lines. I see others caught in pieces of plastic trash.

Over the years, I've found it harder and harder to find sharks anywhere. Because of overfishing and pollution, the oceans' great predators are in danger of dying out completely.

Not long ago, I was asked to join a National Geographic expedition (sounds like eks-puh-DISH-un). The members of the expedition were headed to one of the most remote, or faraway, places on the planet. They said I would see a lot of sharks there. So, of course, I jumped at the chance!

A diver explores a reef in the Line Islands. The reddish orange fish are red snappers. They nipped at our fingers and ears!

In the center of the Pacific Ocean is a chain of 11 islands called the Line Islands. Most of the islands belong to the nation of Kiribati (sounds like KEE-ree-bas). Altogether, fewer than 9,000 people live here. On most of the islands, there are no people at all.

Coral reefs ring each of the islands. Reefs are full of nooks and crannies. These make good homes for many kinds of plants and animals. Coral reefs are like the rain forests of the sea. Of all the different types of ocean fish, a third of them make their homes on or near reefs.

Around the Line Islands, reef life has been undisturbed for hundreds of years. That's why National Geographic scientist Enric Sala (sounds like en-REEK SAL-ah) was eager to see the sharks and other wildlife here. He wanted to study an area still untouched by humans.

It was late in March. I flew to Tahiti (sounds like TUH-hee-tee) and met up with Dr. Sala and his crew. We boarded our research ship. It was called the *Hanse Explorer*. We were thrilled to set sail. All around us was the vast, open ocean.

It took us three days to reach the first of the islands we would be studying. It was a tiny island called Flint. My first dive here was awesome. But I knew we were headed for places even more remote.

On the ninth day, we sailed close to Starbuck Island. The water around Starbuck was too shallow for our ship. So we dropped anchor in the deeper water offshore.

We inflated our small rubber boats. Then we lowered them into the water and hopped in. We paddled to a place that looked good for diving. I grabbed my camera and slipped into the water. I knew we were probably the first people to ever dive here.

This reef was like an enchanted forest! I felt caught up in a swirl of color.

I'd explored many coral reefs in the world, but this reef looked thicker. It looked healthier. Deep green algae grew between the corals. Schools of small fish darted over the corals. They nipped at the algae.

I also saw many large predatory fish, such as grouper and red snapper. Out beyond the reef's edge, I saw big tunas. They rocketed past like silver torpedoes.

Most amazing were the sharks. Absolutely everywhere, I saw sharks! I saw blacktip, whitetip, and gray reef sharks. They patrolled the waters, hunting for their next meal. On most reefs today, you're lucky to see even one or two sharks. To find one, you have to set out bait. You have to lure it in. Here, no bait was needed. Here, sharks ruled!

# Underwater Flying Saucer

A coral may look like a plant, or even like a rock. But it is really a tiny animal called a polyp (sounds like PAH-lup). Polyps have soft bodies with hard outer skeletons. Polyps join together in groups called colonies. The colonies can grow for hundreds of years. A coral reef is a solid structure made of the skeletons of millions of corals. Near one of the Line Islands, Kingman Reef, we discovered a new kind of coral. It had formed a huge, saucer-shaped colony. It is more than 500 years old.

I took photographs of the beautiful underwater landscape. It amazed me to think that no humans had ever seen it before.

Dr. Sala and his crew worked hard. They counted fish and tested the water. They checked the health of the coral. Dr. Sala thinks that ten times more sharks live here than on any other reef on the planet.

Some of the sharks seemed curious about me. They moved in close to check me out. Once they had, they just went about their business.

Those red snappers were a different story, though! They had fearsome, needle-sharp teeth. A few looked me over. It seemed like they wanted a taste. Sometimes I had to push them away with my camera. They pestered all of us. They nipped at our ears and fingers. I had the feeling if I were just a little smaller, they would eat me for lunch!

Back on the ship, we had first aid kits loaded with bandages to put on our fish bites and coral scrapes. Places like Starbuck are so remote, you have to bring everything you need with you. We had packed all kinds of safety gear, too. We also had signaling devices, in case we got lost.

We felt proud that we'd planned everything so well. But we were soon to find out that no matter how well you plan, some things you just can't control.

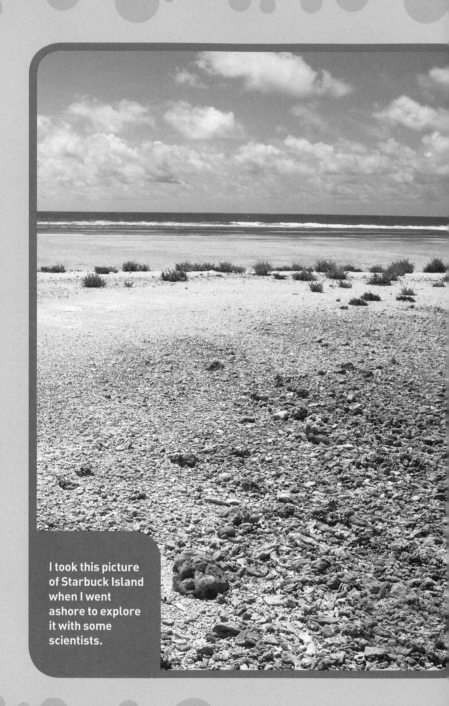

I took this picture of Starbuck Island when I went ashore to explore it with some scientists.

## Chapter 3

# STRANDED!

I'd been diving in the waters off Starbuck for several days. But I wanted to go ashore to take some photos of the land.

Two of the scientists on the expedition were already on the island. They were studying the seabirds of Starbuck. I decided to join them there. Dr. Sala and my assistant Mauricio Handler came along. National Geographic was making a film of our expedition. A couple of the film crew came, too.

Getting from the ship to the island was a challenge. No boat, not even one of our small rubber boats, could get near the shore. The hard, jagged reef would cut the boat to shreds.

There was only one way to get to Starbuck. We had to swim there! Not only that, I had to put my cameras in a watertight case. Mauricio and I had to tow the case with us as we swam. We struggled to keep from being dashed against the reef by the waves. We were

**Did You Know?**

**Giant clams live around the Line Islands. These monster shellfish were once known as man-eating clams. In truth, no clam has ever eaten a person.**

lucky to make it to shore with only a few scrapes and bruises.

Starbuck is very hot and dry. After a few hours of taking photos, we were ready to head back to the ship. But by this time, the sea had changed. Now huge waves were smashing against the shore.

Our captain radioed us. He said it had become too dangerous. There was no way we could swim back to the ship that night. We were stranded! And we had no food, water, or shelter.

The captain had a plan to help us. He kept a rocket gun for just such emergencies. He eased one of the ship's lifeboats as close to the island as he dared. Then he used the gun to shoot a line to shore.

# Hope for Sharks

One of the greatest hopes for sharks are marine protected areas. These are sections of the ocean where fishing is strictly limited. So far, less than 2 percent of the ocean is protected. But many people are working hard to make sure more areas will be protected in the future. Dr. Sala continues to work with the local people and the government of Kiribati. They hope to turn the beautiful reefs of the Line Islands into a new marine protected area.

We grabbed the line. On the other end of it, our shipmates attached a waterproof box. It was filled with food, water bottles, and a plastic tarp. We hauled the box through the waves. We hoped it would not smash against the reef and break. Lucky for us, it made it in one piece!

With the tarp and some wood we found on the beach, we built a small shelter. We huddled under it. We were exhausted, hungry, and sunburned. Soon, heavy rain began to pour down. We lay awake most of the night. We wondered what the morning would bring.

As the sun came up, the waves seemed to have calmed down a bit. We decided we would each swim back to the ship with a buddy or two. That way we could help each other if we got into trouble.

But first, we watched the waves. We needed to get an idea of how often the really big ones came in. When we saw a lull, or pause, in the waves, we would swim fast through the shallow water over the dangerous reef. Once we were in the deeper water, we'd be safe.

My swim buddy and I saw a lull in the waves. So she and I began to swim out. Then she hesitated. I turned back to help her. As we tried to make our way through the shallows, I saw a giant wave coming toward us. I shouted for her to put her head down and swim as hard as she could! I took a deep breath and dove under the wave. But not so far under that I would crash against the coral!

We had to dive beneath a couple more of those big waves. Then, finally, we were past the danger zone.

Exhausted and out of breath, we climbed aboard our ship. Everyone made it back safely. As we sailed on to our next stop, we all felt very lucky.

Based on Dr. Sala's studies of the Line Islands, we now have a clearer picture of what a healthy reef looks like. One thing we have learned is that a healthy reef supports lots of sharks and other predatory fish. Understanding the reefs here will help us figure out how to restore reefs that have been polluted and overfished.

I knew that exploring a remote location like Starbuck would be dangerous. But having a chance to take photos in a place few humans ever go is the stuff of dreams. I hope my photos will let people see the beauty of these amazing reefs and get a better understanding of sharks. I hope they'll be inspired to help protect sharks and their wild ocean habitats, all around the world.

THE END

# INDEX

# MORE INFORMATION

To find more information about the animal species featured in this book, check out these books and websites.

*National Geographic Kids Everything Sharks,* by Ruth A. Musgrave, National Geographic, 2011

*Ocean Soul,* by Brian Skerry, National Geographic, 2011

*A Whale on Her Own,* by Brian Skerry, Blackbirch Press, 2000

National Geographic "Animals: Coral"
animals.nationalgeographic.com/animals/
invertebrates/coral

National Geographic "Animals: Sharks"
animals.nationalgeographic.com/animals/sharks

National Geographic Kids "Creature Features: Belugas"
kids.nationalgeographic.com/kids/animals/
creaturefeature/belugas

National Geographic Kids "Creature Features: Harp Seals"
kids.nationalgeographic.com/kids/animals/
creaturefeature/harp-seals

National Geographic Kids "Creature Features: Leatherback Sea Turtles"
kids.nationalgeographic.com/kids/animals/creaturefeature/
leatherback-sea-turtle

For Katherine and Caroline—B. S.

For Geoffrey—K. W. Z.

# CREDITS

Inside This Book TOC: Book 2, Whale Who Won Hearts:
All photos by Brian Skerry; Title page, Brian Skerry; All interior
photos are by Brian Skerry unless noted here: 19, William West/
AFP/Getty Images; 72, Flip Nicklin/Minden Pictures; 101, © IFAW/
WTI S. Kadur; 102, © IFAW/WTI A. Mookerjee.

# ACKNOWLEDGMENTS

I am most grateful to *National Geographic* magazine for commis-
sioning me to produce photographs and stories. I especially wish
to thank Editor in Chief Chris Johns, Director of Photography Sarah
Leen, Deputy Director of Photography Ken Geiger, and Senior
Editor for Natural History Kathy Moran for their support of my work.

So much of my work relies on the expertise of dedicated profes-
sionals from many disciplines in locations worldwide. Assisting
me with the projects written about in this book are the following
people, to whom I give great thanks: Scott Benson, Barbara Block,
Mario Cyr, Scott Eckert, Mike Hammill, Mauricio Handler, Mike
James, Jim Johnson, Rod Mast, Tom Mulloy, Enric Sala, Becky
Sjare, Kelly Stewart, Sean Whelan, and Jeff Wildermuth.

Finally, I wish to thank my wife, Marcia, and daughters, Kate and
Caroline, for their loving support and inspiration. — *Brian Skerry*

# LUCKY LEOPARDS!

## And More True Stories of Amazing Animal Rescues

Aline Alexander Newman

**Published by the National Geographic Society**
John M. Fahey, *Chairman of the Board and Chief Executive Officer*
Declan Moore, *Executive Vice President; President, Publishing and Travel*
Melina Gerosa Bellows, *Executive Vice President; Chief Creative Officer, Books, Kids, and Family*

**Prepared by the Book Division**
Hector Sierra, *Senior Vice President and General Manager*
Nancy Laties Feresten, *Senior Vice President, Kids Publishing and Media*
Jay Sumner, *Director of Photography, Children's Publishing*
Jennifer Emmett, *Vice President, Editorial Director, Children's Books*
Eva Absher-Schantz, *Design Director, Kids Publishing and Media*
R. Gary Colbert, *Production Director*
Jennifer A. Thornton, *Director of Managing Editorial*

**Staff for This Book**
Becky Baines, *Project Editor*
Eva Absher-Schantz, *Art Director*
Kelley Miller, *Senior Photo Editor*
Ruthie Thompson, *Designer*
Ariane Szu-Tu, *Editorial Assistant*
Callie Broaddus, *Design Production Assistant*
Grace Hill, *Associate Managing Editor*
Joan Gossett, *Production Editor*
Marfé Ferguson Delano, *Release Editor*
Lewis R. Bassford, *Production Manager*
Susan Borke, *Legal and Business Affairs*
Jennifer Raichek, *Intern*

**Production Services**
Phillip L. Schlosser, *Senior Vice President*
Chris Brown, *Vice President, NG Book Manufacturing*
George Bounelis, *Vice President, Production Services*
Nicole Elliott, *Manager*
Rachel Faulise, *Manager*
Robert L. Barr, *Manager*

The National Geographic Society is one of the world's largest nonprofit scientific and educational organizations. Founded in 1888 to "increase and diffuse geographic knowledge," the Society's mission is to inspire people to care about the planet. It reaches more than 400 million people worldwide each month through its official journal, *National Geographic*, and other magazines; National Geographic Channel; television documentaries; music; radio; films; books; DVDs; maps; exhibitions; live events; school publishing programs; interactive media; and merchandise. National Geographic has funded more than 10,000 scientific research, conservation, and exploration projects and supports an education program promoting geographic literacy.

For more information, please visit www.nationalgeographic.com, call 1-800-NGS LINE (647-5463), or write to the following address:
National Geographic Society
1145 17th Street N.W.
Washington, D.C. 20036-4688 U.S.A.

Visit us online at nationalgeographic.com/books

For librarians and teachers:
ngchildrensbooks.org

National Geographic supports K–12 educators with ELA Common Core Resources. Visit natgeoed.org/commoncore for more information.

More for kids from National Geographic:
kids.nationalgeographic.com

For information about special discounts for bulk purchases, please contact National Geographic Books Special Sales:
ngspecsales@ngs.org

For rights or permissions inquiries, please contact National Geographic Books Subsidiary Rights: ngbookrights@ngs.org

Trade paperback
ISBN: 978-1-4263-1457-5
Reinforced library edition
ISBN: 978-1-4263-1458-2

# Table of CONTENTS

Runa and Kata explore the forest. Their spotted coats blend in with the leaves.

# RUNA
# AND KATA:
# LUCKY
# LEOPARDS

Runa and Kata nuzzle each other. They are as soft and cuddly as pet kittens.

## Chapter 1

## March 2009, Assam, India

People watched their step in the Assam (sounds like ah-SAHM) jungle in northeast India. Roads were few and made of dirt. Trees grew so close together they almost touched. And bushy plants and fallen logs covered the forest floor. You never knew when a hungry tiger or slithering python might surprise you. This place was wild. It belonged to the animals.

Two of those animals lay sleeping in a hollow tree. They were newborn kittens, or cubs. Their mother had left them alone while she went hunting for food. The cubs should have been safe. Except before the mama returned, some woodcutters came.

The woodcutters lived in a village on the edge of the forest, in a part of India called Kokrajhar (sounds like co-kruh-JAR). They earned money by gathering firewood to sell. One man saw the hollow tree. He chopped it down with his ax. The tree landed with a thud. Then he got a big surprise.

Two tiny furballs bounced out! The startled woodcutter dropped his ax. He scooped up the tiny cats. They mewed softly. Their gray spotted coats felt as soft as a baby chick. *What are they?* the man wondered. *Baby tigers or baby leopards?*

It didn't matter. The cubs were adorable. And there was no danger in picking them up. The babies' eyes hadn't even opened yet. *If only I could sell these cats*, he thought.

The woodcutter was very poor. He knew that wild-animal dealers would pay big money for the cubs. Then the dealers would sell the cubs for even more money. Rich collectors from other countries paid thousands of dollars for wild animals to put in their backyard zoos.

Even if no dealers came along, the cubs were a good find. Maybe the woodcutter could sell them as pets. Or his neighbors might buy them. Some men tied animal parts to their swords. This was a custom, or tradition, in his village. Some people hung animal skins up to decorate their huts. Local healers also used animal parts to make medicine.

The woodcutter knew it was wrong to capture wild animals. It was wrong to sell them too. The Indian government had laws against these things. But the thought of all the money he could make dazzled him. What if he could make $200 selling the cubs? That would be like winning the lottery! With that much money he could feed his family for many months.

The woodcutter carried the cubs home. Then he quietly spread the word. He had jungle cats for sale.

But his plan went wrong. He didn't know how to take care of the cubs. He didn't know how to feed them. Or even what to feed them! Another villager became worried. He told a forest department worker named Akhim (sounds like ah-KEEM) about the cubs. Akhim went to the woodcutter. He demanded the kittens. The woodcutter turned them over.

Akhim rushed the baby cats to the local wildlife rescue center. It was run by the Wildlife Trust of India. It was not a moment too soon. The cubs hadn't eaten in days. "One of them was seriously sick," says Sonali Ghosh (sounds like so-NAH-lee GOUSH). Sonali is an officer with the Indian Forest Service. "I was scared it might die," she said.

The rescue center veterinarians (sounds like vet-er-ih-NARE-ee-ens) examined the baby cats. "These are common leopards," the vets decided. The common leopard is the kind most "commonly" seen. There are also snow leopards, clouded leopards, and Sunda clouded leopards.

Everyone at the rescue center treated the cubs with great care. Workers fed the kittens around the clock. They gave them goat's milk, using baby bottles.

Leopards are meat-eaters. So the vets wanted the cubs to get a taste for meat. After about three weeks, the workers started mixing liver soup in with the goat's milk.

The cubs ate a lot. They grew fast. As they got bigger, the markings on their coats became easier to see. One day the vets noticed something very interesting. The spots on these cubs looked different from the spots on common leopards. They were darker and grayer.

The vets looked at each other. They wondered . . .

Could it be?

Yes! These cubs weren't common leopards after all. They were clouded leopards. Extremely rare, almost never seen, clouded leopards!

**Did You Know?**

As babies, clouded leopards have blue eyes. Later their eyes turn yellow.

# Which Is Which?

Clouded leopards and common leopards are both big cats. But they are not the same kind, or species (sounds like SPEE-sheez), of cat. They are as different from each other as lions are from tigers.

## COMMON LEOPARDS

- Live in forests, plains, deserts, and mountains in parts of Africa, Central Asia, India, and China.
- Roar loudly.
- Weigh up to 106 pounds (48 kg).
- Are covered with small, dark-colored, round spots.
- Have feet that always face front.

**COMMON LEOPARD**

**CLOUDED LEOPARD**

# CLOUDED LEOPARDS

- Live in tropical forests in Southeast Asia and India.
- Purr and meow.
- Weigh up to 50 pounds (22.7 kg).
- Are covered with large spots that look like brown and gray clouds.
- Can turn their hind feet so they face backward.

The higher the better for clouded leopard cubs! They play, eat, and rest up in the treetops.

## Chapter 2

# A BOLD PLAN

Clouded leopards are very shy. They spend a lot of their time high up in trees. They are rarely seen in the wild.

The fact that these rescued cubs were clouded leopards changed everything. If they had been common leopards, the vets would have had to send them to a zoo. It's the law in India. That's because hand-raised common leopards lose their fear of humans. They might attack people if they were set free.

But clouded leopards don't bother humans. They hang out in treetops. Releasing hand-raised clouded leopards back into the wild would be OK. It would not put humans at risk.

But could these animals make it without their mother? Could they learn to protect themselves? Could they find their own food?

Bhaskar Choudhury (sounds like bas-CAR CHOW-durry) thought they could. So did Ian Robinson. Bhaskar is a veterinarian with the Wildlife Trust of India (WTI). Ian is the animal rescue director at the International Fund for Animal Welfare (IFAW). There was only one problem. IFAW had successfully released hand-raised elephants, bears, and even a tiger. But not a clouded leopard. No one had ever tried doing that.

The animal experts at WTI talked to the people at IFAW. They discussed what needed to be done. They talked about what could go wrong. Guess what? They decided to go for it! Everyone was super-excited to help save these rare animals.

Bhaskar and another vet, Panjit Basumatary (sounds like pan-JEET bo-SOM-uh-terry), went right to work. They put up a large cage out in the yard. They put blankets inside the cage for the cubs to sleep on. They also put branches inside it for the cubs to climb on.

Both of the cubs were males. The vets named one of them Runa (sounds like

RU-nuh). They called the other cub Kata (sounds like co-TAH).

The cubs had a lot to learn. After a few weeks, the vets started feeding them small chunks of cooked meat. Ian liked the cubs' reaction. "They would grab a piece of food and climb up in the branches to eat it," he says. "Climbing was instinctive [sounds like in-STINK-tiv] for them." In other words, they were born climbers.

The next step was getting them to eat their meat raw. That's what leopards do in the wild. So the vets began tossing dead chickens into the cubs' cage. Soon the cubs were eating plenty of raw meat.

In September 2009, Runa and Kata turned seven months old. They were big and healthy. They were eating well. It was time for them to learn clouded leopard ways. It was time to move them back to the jungle. But would the experiment work? Nobody knew.

Three men from Kokrajhar served as the cubs' keepers in the forest. They lived in huts they built themselves. The huts were high above the ground. Each one was fitted between four trees. The huts had a bamboo floor, roof, and walls.

It was not easy work. Countless insects buzzed and whined all day and all night. They flew into the men's eyes and bit their skin. Cobras and other deadly snakes hid under bushes.

## Mystery Cat

Clouded leopards are so seldom seen that scientists know very little about them. Here's what they do know:

1. Clouded leopards have very long tails, which help them balance on tree branches.
2. They use their hind feet to hang upside down from tree branches.
3. They eat birds, monkeys, pigs, small deer, and porcupines.
4. They ambush prey by leaping onto their backs and biting their necks.
5. They are good swimmers.
6. They are called "mint leopards" in China and "tree tigers" in Malaysia.

The keepers also faced danger from prowling tigers and charging elephants. That's why they put their huts up high—to stay out of the animals' reach.

For nine long months, the keepers lived like this. "These men were dedicated to these cubs," says Ian. "And brave. This was a tough job."

The keepers took turns, so that two men were on duty at the same time. The third would have the week off to return to the village for food and supplies.

Runa and Kata also slept in the treetops. They needed to be safe from tigers and elephants, too. Their keepers lashed bamboo poles together and built a platform high off the ground. They built a ladder the same way. Then they set a large green cage on top of the platform. The cage was made of metal and wire. It had a swinging door that locked. The keepers climbed up the ladder each night and locked the cubs inside.

During the day the keepers took the cubs for long walks on the ground. They walked them each morning and evening. The keepers kept the cubs on a leash at first. This way the cubs slowly got used to the sights, sounds, and smells of the forest.

At first the young leopards were scared. This was natural and to be expected. But after a week, the keepers let the cubs loose. They expected them to run around exploring. Instead, Runa and Kata acted like pet dogs. They stuck close to their keepers.

The vets and keepers began to worry. "The animal that goes off and cares nothing for you when he goes is most successful," says Ian. Had these cubs become too fond of people?

If so, that was bad news. Humans are the clouded leopard's biggest enemy. They hunt and trap the cats for their fur and bones. If these cubs liked people, they would leave the forest. They would hang around the villages looking for food and friendship. That kind of behavior would get them killed.

Raising these clouded leopards had been a grand experiment. But now it seemed they had failed. Bhaskar, Ian, and the others felt like a big black cloud had settled over their heads.

One of the twins peers through the bushes. His black markings, pink nose, and white muzzle look painted on.

## Chapter 3

# TOUGH LOVE

The cubs' forest keepers knew they had to do something. They decided to change their behavior toward the cubs. One day Kata stopped walking to scratch his nails on a fallen log. Afterward he rubbed against his keeper like a house cat.

The keeper sighed. His heart told him to pet and snuggle Kata. But his head told him he must not.

Not if he wanted the cat to stay in the wild. Not if he wanted Kata to survive! The keeper knew Kata needed to become independent. So Kata's faithful human friend forced himself to do something very hard. He turned Kata around and pushed him away.

Again and again the keepers did this. Soon the plan seemed to be working. The cubs began grabbing chunks of food and scrambling up a tree. The keepers were pleased. At least they were until the cats shot straight up a towering tree trunk. They climbed so high that the keepers had to crane their necks to see them. Now what? Would the spunky daredevils suddenly turn into scaredy cats? Would they be afraid to come down?

Not to worry. The clouded leopards simply turned their bodies and spun their hind feet around. They dug their sharp claws into the tree's bark. And bingo! They raced headfirst to the ground!

What a neat trick! Squirrels can do that. But tigers can't. Neither can lions or common leopards. Clouded leopards are the only big cats that can.

Runa and Kata gradually learned their way around the forest. So their keepers let them stay loose for longer. But the keepers still followed the cats everywhere they went. If the cubs disappeared, their keepers whistled. The cats ran back.

How to travel through the forest was not all these furry twins needed to learn. They also needed to learn to hunt.

In the wild, clouded leopard mamas bring their babies food to eat. Supper is often a golden langur (sounds like LANG-goor) monkey. Monkeys live in the trees and are easy to find. But clouded leopards also eat birds, squirrels, snakes, lizards, and big juicy insects.

As adults, clouded leopards must catch their own food. But how do they know how to do it? Do they learn by watching? Or are they born with the ability and develop it over time? Scientists are not exactly sure. "We believed that the skill of hunting was born in them," Ian says.

If he was right, the cubs could make it in the wild. If he was wrong, they would have to live in a zoo. It was time to find out.

Runa and Kata were full-grown now. In the wild, adult clouded leopards are nocturnal (sounds like nok-TUR-nul). This means they sleep during the day and hunt and prowl at night. The keepers decided to keep the twins' cage door open all the time. Now the leopards could explore whenever they wanted.

Runa and Kata started staying out later and later. But they still returned to their cage to eat. "Feeding was very rough-and-tumble," Ian says. "The cubs had to be fed in separate corners. Otherwise they would fight and steal each other's food." This went on for months. Would the leopards ever learn to hunt for themselves?

One day, a stray chicken wandered into the forest. Runa spied it and grabbed the bird by the neck. But he didn't kill it. A minute later he let it go. Still, he had taken an important first step.

The next chicken that crossed Runa's path was not so lucky. "These cats were always on the edge of their nerves," says Ian. "They were so alert and aware of the slightest sound." This chicken barely entered the forest before feathers flew. Both leopards attacked the hen. They wrestled for it. They bit. They snarled and hissed. Kata finally won the prize. Then he carried his supper straight up a tree.

Clouded leopards are the only big cats that spend so much time in trees. As Runa and Kata started to do this, they spent less time with their keepers.

Weeks passed. The leopards stayed away

longer and longer. They stopped playing with their keepers. They focused on each other instead. Runa and Kata now behaved less like pets and more like wild animals.

Then something happened that sealed the deal. In May 2010, a stray dog trotted into the forest. The keepers saw the dog coming. But they were too far away to help. All they could do was hold their breath and hope for the best.

And then it happened.

Runa and Kata teamed up and attacked the dog!

It might seem sad, but in the jungle, "kill or be killed" is a way of life. The big cats were just following their instincts.

And that's exactly what the keepers were waiting to see. Now they knew their job was done. Runa and Kata could defend themselves. They could catch their own food. And they could find their way in the forest. The keepers told Ian, Bhaskar, and Panjit that it was time to let the young cats go.

The vets came. They gave Runa and Kata medicine that put them to sleep. Then the vets put white radio-tracking collars on the cats. This way they could track them to see if they survived. If they did, the vets could release other rescued clouded leopard cubs.

Life in the wild is dangerous for clouded leopards. It is for all animals. But Runa and Kata were lucky. They got a second chance.

They were free!

# One Year Later

Were the clouded leopard cubs still alive? A year after Runa and Kata were released, animal experts returned to the jungle to find out. Things looked bad at first. There were no signals from the radio collars. Elephants had destroyed the cubs' treetop cage.

But the experts kept searching. Days later, they found fresh paw prints. They found clouded leopard poop. They saw scratch marks on a tree. Then they met a forestry worker. He had seen a big spotted cat wearing a white collar. These were all very good signs that the cubs had survived!

Koa lies flat on the shore. He has an injured eye, can't move, and looks dead.

# KOA: TURTLE IN TROUBLE

Like all green turtles, Koa has a heart-shaped shell. It's made up of flattened bones.

# WRONG-WAY SEA TURTLE

## June 18, 2012, northern Oregon

**A** male green sea turtle needed help. He was stuck on a sandy beach along the coast. Healthy male turtles live their entire lives at sea. But this poor guy had washed in on the tide. Now he lay still. Hungry seagulls swooped and shrieked (sounds like SHREEKT) overhead. One gull had already pecked at one of the turtle's eyes.

Nobody knows where this turtle came from. Nobody knows how he landed in Oregon. Graceful swimmers like him normally live in warm tropical oceans. This fellow might have started out in warm water near Mexico. It may be that he got caught in a current. Then the fast-moving ocean water carried him north. The ocean is colder up there.

Sea turtles often ride warm ocean currents halfway around the world. But if the water turns cold, their muscles stop working. They become paralyzed (sounds like PAIR-uh-lized). The turtles can't move. They can't feed and they can't escape. This is called being "cold-stunned."

Nadine Fuller was not feeling her best either. She had been hiking and camping in California with her children and grandchildren. The family had had a wonderful time. But 70-year-old Nadine was tired. She was exhausted from lugging a backpack and all her gear.

Now she was driving back home to Forks, Washington. It was five in the afternoon. She had 800 miles (1,287 km) to go. So Nadine decided to stop for the night in Newport, Oregon. The Moolack Shores Motel there is one of her favorite places.

Nadine pulled into a parking space at the motel. Then she walked inside. "Hi, Frank," she said to the man behind the desk. "Do you have any rooms available? I'd like one for tonight."

Franklin Brooks smiled and nodded. He offered her a plate of cookies. Nadine nibbled on one while Frank checked her in. They chatted a bit. Then Nadine climbed the stairs to her room. She unlocked the door and stepped inside. She dropped her bags on the floor. She opened sliding glass doors to a balcony overlooking the ocean. "Ahh," she sighed.

Nadine breathed in the salty air and gazed out to sea. She listened to the waves pounding the shore. She looked at the Newport lighthouse across the bay. In a few hours, its light would come on. It had been a warm, sunny day. Nadine planned to settle down in a comfy deck chair and enjoy the view. Later she would watch

> **Did You Know?**
>
> **Sea turtles have lived in Earth's oceans for about 150 million years.**

the sun set over the ocean. She was ready
to relax!

But while she was still standing, Nadine
spotted something strange lying on the
beach. It was bigger than a kitchen sink.
"I thought it was a rock, at first," she says.
"But something about it did not look right."

Nadine went back inside her room.
She unpacked the binoculars she always
brings on trips. She held them to her eyes
and adjusted the focus.

*Wow!* It was a sea turtle!

Nadine volunteers with an
environmental (sounds like in-vi-run-
MENT-ul) group called Beachwatchers.
She patrols the beach near her home
once a month looking for dead birds.
If she finds any, she reports them to

Beachwatchers. A rise in numbers tells the group there has been an oil spill or some other disaster in or near the ocean. Nadine had spotted many kinds of birds over the years. She had seen puffins, cormorants (sounds like KORM-er-ents), loons, and albatross (sounds like AL-buh-tross).

She also had seen sea turtles swimming in the ocean off California. But she had never seen a sea turtle this far north. And she had never seen one stranded, or stuck, on shore. "Suddenly, I wasn't tired anymore," says Nadine. Clutching her binoculars, she scurried down the stairs and out onto the beach.

But when Nadine reached the turtle her joy faded. The animal wasn't moving.

Nadine walked all around the turtle.

# Race to the Sea

The most dangerous time in a green turtle's life is right after it hatches. That's because green turtle mothers don't protect their young. They simply drag themselves up on a beach, dig a hole, and lay 100 to 200 eggs. The turtle moms cover the eggs with sand. Then they return to the ocean.

The eggs hatch all at once. The first thing the newborn turtles do is scramble toward the water. Along the way, birds and crabs eat many of them. But those that do make it to the ocean can live for 80 years.

She snapped several pictures of it. Then she gently scraped the sand from the creature's face with a stick. "He blinked one eye," she says. "But I thought that was only a reflex. I thought the turtle was dead."

Some people might have tried to put the turtle back in the water. But Nadine remembered her training. Beachwatchers had taught her to report and not touch.

She knew better than to try to do anything herself. She hurried back to the motel.

"Frank," she cried to the innkeeper. "I found a sea turtle lying on the beach!" She showed him the photos on her digital camera.

**Did You Know?**

Green turtles sometimes crawl out of the water to sunbathe on land.

Frank looked wide-eyed. "I know the head of marine mammal stranding," he said. "His office is only three miles from here."

Frank dialed Jim Rice's cell phone. But Jim was not at his office. He was home cooking supper when his cell phone rang.

"There's a dead turtle on the beach," Frank told him.

Jim felt sad that the turtle had died. But a dead animal was no reason to hurry. Jim figured he could take his time. He finished fixing supper for his ten-year-old son. He ate a bit himself. His wife arrived home. And then, *rrring!* His phone rang again.

"You know that turtle I told you about?" Frank said. "Well, it just moved!"

Randy Getman carries Koa up the stairs from the beach. Jim Rice (left) and Franklin Brooks (right) help.

## Chapter 2

**HURRY! HURRY!**

Jim Rice switched into emergency mode. "There are seven species of sea turtles," he says. "And they are all endangered." This means that they are so few in number that they may one day become extinct. "If we find a live sea turtle," Jim says, "we do everything we can to get him back out there."

It was seven at night when Jim

rushed out the door. Sunset comes late in June. Maybe he could still rescue the turtle before dark. But he had to hurry.

Jim drove to the beach. He swung his car into the parking lot and ran down to the sand. Frank was standing there beside a large turtle. Jim approached the turtle and lightly touched its neck. The turtle's head twitched. Frank had been right. This turtle was alive.

Jim was a marine mammal researcher at Hatfield Marine Science Center. He spent his days studying dead animals found on Oregon's beaches. Most of these were whales, seals, sea lions, or porpoises. It was Jim's job to figure out why they died.

Before moving out west, Jim had worked in Massachusetts. He rescued and helped hundreds of sea turtles recover there. He was a sea turtle expert. But he had not rescued a single one since moving to Oregon. All the turtles Jim worked on there were dead.

Jim examined the turtle's eyes. They looked sunken in. This was a sure sign of dehydration (sounds like de-hi-DRAY-shun). This means the animal didn't have enough water in his body. Green turtles do not drink water. They get all the liquid they need from the food they eat. But this turtle couldn't dive or feed. He was paralyzed. Jim could tell the animal was cold-stunned.

The turtle was in very bad shape. Two more hours on the beach, and he would die for sure. "I faced a challenge," Jim says. "It was getting darker. And the tide was coming in. Somehow we had to beat it." Otherwise, the rushing water would sweep the helpless turtle back out to sea. It would surely drown.

Jim also faced another problem. He didn't have his work truck with him. His work truck had big tires. Big tires would let him drive on the sandy beach. But all he had was his station wagon. Driving to work to fetch his truck would take too long. It would be dark when he returned. And it would be high tide.

So how was he going to get this big animal off the beach? Jim and Frank were discussing what to do when Randy Getman appeared. Randy was the general manager at the Moolack Shores Motel.

He was big and strong, and he loved animals. Randy had an idea. "I'll carry him to your car," he said.

"You'll what?" said Jim. "This turtle must weigh 130 pounds [59 kg]. You'll hurt your back."

Randy shook his head. "I can do it," he insisted.

So Jim called James Burke. James is director of animal husbandry (sounds like HUZ-ben-dree) at the Oregon Coast Aquarium. Jim told James about the turtle and asked if the aquarium had room for him. "Of course," James said. "I'll meet you there."

**Did You Know?**

Green turtles eat jellyfish. This surprised scientists. Until 2009, they thought these turtles ate only plants.

# Turtle Trivia

## GREEN SEA TURTLES

- Have flippers instead of legs. The bones in their flippers look like the bones in your hands.
- Cannot pull their heads inside their shells.
- Can stay underwater for hours without coming up to breathe.
- Have no teeth.
- Weigh up to 500 pounds (227 kg).
- Swim very fast, up to 20 miles (32 km) an hour.
- Have brown or black shells. They get their name from the green-colored fat inside their bodies.

Jim put his phone away. He and Randy stood on opposite sides of the turtle. They gripped his shell and lifted him up. Frank stood behind, holding some of the weight. The three men carried the turtle down the beach and up the first set of stairs. But then the stairs narrowed. The men could no longer walk side by side. They set the turtle down and rested a few minutes.

Then Randy bent over. "Put him on," he said.

Jim and Frank lifted the turtle onto Randy's back. They draped the turtle's flippers over Randy's strong shoulders. And Randy piggybacked the turtle up two more flights of stairs.

In the parking lot, Jim opened his car's hatchback. He and Frank lifted the turtle off Randy's shoulders and set him inside. Jim shut the hatch, hopped in the driver's seat, and headed to the aquarium. The fishy stink of turtle grew stronger as he drove.

Jim called James Burke again on the way. "We'll be there in ten minutes," he said.

When Jim and the turtle arrived, James was waiting at the door. He and Jim unloaded the turtle and carried him into a large, warehouse-type building. Inside the building sat different-size water tanks. The men found an empty one and laid the turtle inside. They propped the edges of his shell on foam pads to keep weight off his lungs. That way his chest could go in and out with every breath.

Big as the turtle was, he was too weak to put up a fight. That made him easy to handle. Jim and James knew what to do, and they worked quickly. First they checked the turtle over. Could he move his flippers and blink his eyes? Barely. They weighed the turtle and washed the few wounds he had. Then they took his temperature (sounds like TEM-preh-chur). Next, they drew blood and injected fluids into the turtle's body.

"It was pretty intense," says James. "This turtle belonged to an endangered species. If we saved him, and put him back in the wild, we'd help his whole species survive."

But could he be saved?

The two men did not know. All they could do was try their hardest. The rest was up to nature . . . and the turtle.

Green turtles swim fast. They can zip along at 20 miles (32 km) an hour.

## Chapter 3

# SWIM AWAY HOME

At first, it was touch and go. James Burke kept the turtle dry. He took his temperature daily. He wanted the turtle's body temperature, or temp, to match the air temp of the room. It took two weeks for that to happen. When it did, James added a little water to the tank. Then he began raising the water temp. He set it two degrees higher each day.

At last James got the turtle's body temp up to 75°F (24°C). That was a nice, healthy temp.

James and his co-workers had to get the turtle eating next. They fed him water plants called algae (sounds like AL-jee). They also fed him a kind of seaweed called bull kelp. They gave the turtle tiny bits at first.

"We were very careful," says James. "Sea turtles get tossed around in the surf. They get water in their lungs. So they often suffer from pneumonia [sounds like nu-MOAN-yuh.]" That's a lung sickness. A rescued turtle can seem to get

**Did You Know?**

Green sea turtle eggs are the size of Ping-Pong balls. Newly hatched turtles are about two inches (5 cm) long.

better. Then it can suddenly die of the disease. James had seen it happen.

In time, the keepers moved the turtle to a larger tank. Then they began dropping more algae into the water for him to munch on. "By week three, things were starting to look really good," James says. "This guy just wasn't giving up."

The keepers grew fond of the big reptile. One of them named him Koa (sounds like CO-uh). Koa is a Hawaiian word. It means strong and fearless.

By August 21, Koa had gained 28 pounds (13 kg). He acted very lively now. James knew he could be returned to the ocean. But not in Oregon. The water there was much too cold. Koa needed to go south. But where? And how?

James called the United States Fish and Wildlife Service. Together they decided that San Diego, California, looked good. It was 780 miles (1,255 km) to the south. The ocean temp there was in the high 70s (about 25°C) in the summer. And SeaWorld San Diego was there. SeaWorld helped many sick and hurt marine animals get well. They had the equipment and know-how for the job. Plus, the United States Navy had an airbase in San Diego. Maybe they could help. And that's exactly what they did.

A Navy plane flew from San Diego to Eugene (sounds like yu-JEEN), Oregon. On board were two animal keepers from SeaWorld. Koa was waiting for them at the airport. He was in a large wooden crate.

# Where Did All the Turtles Go?

Five hundred years ago, the ocean near Florida teemed with turtles. There were so many that one sailor said the ocean "seemed to be full of little rocks." Then over the years things changed. People stole turtle eggs. Large fishing nets captured turtles by accident. People put buildings over beaches where turtles nested. Green turtles began to disappear.

In 1978, scientists listed green turtles as endangered. And people took action! Florida set aside 30.5 miles (49 km) of beach just for turtles. Today more green turtles nest there than anywhere else in the United States.

The crate was handmade by workers at the Oregon Coast Aquarium. On it were stickers reading "This Side Up." It was lined with foam-rubber padding. Twenty airholes were drilled in its sides. Each airhole was as big as a silver dollar.

When the plane set down at the airport in Eugene, a crowd was waiting. Everyone wanted to see what the Navy and SeaWorld called "Operation Turtle Lift." Reporters were there with cameras and recorders. Even Nadine Fuller was there. She was excited to see the turtle she had found. The last time she saw him he was near death. Now he was healthy again. It gave Nadine a good feeling to know that Koa would be released to cruise around the seaweed again.

She watched the keepers load Koa on board. Then the plane lifted off. "Good luck," she whispered. "I'm glad I was the one to find and help you."

Most stranded sea turtles need a full year of care. But Koa got well fast. By the end of September, he was ready to be released. The only problem left was the time of year. It was fall. The ocean was cold. But in October, the coastal waters turned surprisingly warm. They were warm enough for Koa to survive. His keepers attached a small ID tag to one of his flippers. They wanted to know if he ever washed ashore again.

SeaWorld workers put Koa on a special boat. It had a door in one side. They drove the turtle out to sea. Then they opened the door. They pushed the turtle into the waves. Koa stroked his powerful front flippers and glided away.

The release team cheered.

People in Oregon also cheered. They were glad to hear the good news about Koa. Very few sea turtles strand on the Oregon coast. Even fewer survive. It's just too cold. But there was something odd about 2012. Seven sea turtles stranded in Oregon that year.

"It was the most strandings in a single year that I have on record," says Jim Rice. He doesn't know why. Maybe a freak warm water current brought the turtles north and then suddenly turned cold.

But there is no proof of that. What Jim does know is that Koa is the only one of those seven stranded turtles to survive.

It took months of work. It also took dozens of people: Nadine Fuller, Franklin Brooks, Jim Rice, Randy Getman, James Burke and the staff at the Oregon Coast Aquarium, the U.S. Fish and Wildlife Service, SeaWorld San Diego, and the Navy. Together they gave the plucky green turtle a new life.

Koa's rescuers hope that he will live long. They also hope he will father many thousands of babies. Maybe he will help green sea turtles come off the endangered list. If so, these gentle creatures will continue to fill our oceans. And we will be happier just knowing they are there.

# CROOKED NECK: THE LONE LOON

This loon has caught a fish. Before eating, he'll turn it so it goes down headfirst.

A loon sits on her nest. Most loons use the same nest year after year.

## Chapter 1

# DOUBLE TROUBLE

## July 2009, Old Forge, New York

Few people slowed down long enough to notice. But a bird called a common loon sat on a muddy nest in a busy lake called First Lake. It is one of a chain of lakes in the Adirondack (sounds like Ad-i-RON-dack) Mountains.

The loon had a black head, snow white breast, and white spots on black wings. Inside her nest lay two big, greenish eggs. The eggs were almost ready to hatch.

But before they did, a storm struck. Rain poured down. The water level in the lake quickly rose much higher than normal. Then the sun came out. Waves from passing boats washed over the nest.

The loon and her mate had made a mistake. They had built their nest on a floating bog. A floating bog is a chunk of matted grass, roots, and moss that is not connected to the shore. It looks like a little island, but there's no solid ground. Floating bogs act like sponges. They soak up water.

A loon-watcher named Bob Zimmerman knew about the nest. He grew concerned when the waters rose. So he jumped into his canoe and paddled over to check. *Oh, no!* he thought. Bob rushed back to camp—which is what he calls his summer home near the lake—and called Gary Lee. Gary is a retired forest ranger and an expert on birds.

"We have some loons here that need your help," Bob said. "Their nest is flooded!"

"I'll be right there," Gary said. He raced outside. Sitting out in his yard was a nesting platform he had built for emergencies. It was made of unsinkable cedar logs, Styrofoam (STI-ruh-foam), and plastic mesh. Gary lifted the platform into the back of his pickup truck. He drove to Bob's camp.

Gary knew he didn't have much time. If a little water seeps into their nest, loon eggs can survive for a short while. But more than a half inch (1.3 cm) of water will chill the eggs, and the chicks will die.

When Gary reached Bob's camp, he found Bob and his son-in-law waiting for him. The three men hopped into Bob's rowboat and rowed to the nest. The sight of them frightened the mother loon. "She panicked," Gary says. She slid headfirst into the water and watched the goings-on from a short distance away.

Gary and Bob climbed out of the boat and onto the floating bog. It sank. Cold water rose to their waists. Gary snatched up the eggs and handed them to the man in the boat. "Keep them warm," he said.

Gary and Bob quickly pulled the loons' soggy nesting material off the bog. Then

Gary pressed the nest back together on top of his homemade platform. He tied the platform to two cement blocks and dropped it in the water. He returned the eggs to the nest. Then the men hurried away.

Mama loon jumped right back on her nest. A few days later, *hooray!* Her chicks hatched!

**Did You Know?**

**Loon chicks can swim as soon as they hatch.**

By December, the pair of loons and their youngsters had left the lake. This is normal. Loons migrate. They spend winters in the ocean and return to the same northern lakes each spring.

The mama loon and her mate had been coming to First Lake for several years. So had Neil and Aline Newman.

# The Lowdown on Loons

1. In summer, loons live on northern lakes from Maine to Alaska. They winter in the oceans.
2. Loons eat fish, frogs, and bugs.
3. Loons need a runway. They beat their wings and run across the water for as long as four football fields in order to take off.
4. Loons can fly more than 75 miles (121 km) an hour.
5. Loons wail, hoot, and make a sound like crazy laughter. Each male also has a special call that is all his own.

They had a camp nearby. Every year they watched for the loons to return. The male loon always arrived first. Sometimes they spotted him on the water. Other times they heard his spooky cry. *"Aaaaahhhhhhooooooo!"* he would wail, calling for his mate. Aline and Neil would always stop what they were doing and listen.

Now it was a warm afternoon in September 2011. Aline and Neil were boating on the lake. Aline spotted the mother loon on the water. Her mate and a new pair of chicks drifted beside her.

"Look," Aline said. "Our loons are out." Neil followed her gaze and smiled.

The adult birds looked handsome as always. But there was something odd about the youngsters. One chick looked smaller than the other. Loon eggs only hatch a day apart. So the chicks should have been about the same size. Neil and Aline didn't think much about it at first. They were too busy enjoying their pontoon (sounds like pon-TOON) boat.

A pontoon is a flat-bottomed boat built on top of metal tubes. It's like a raft. Aline had packed books, soft drinks, crackers, and cheese. It was a perfect day to lie in the sun and read.

Neil cut the motor and dropped anchor. They watched the loons while they ate. Every so often the parents poked their heads underwater and scanned for fish. When they saw one, they'd dive and grab it. One of the chicks was doing the same. But the other just floated along.

This worried Neil. "Why doesn't the smallest loon dive?" he asked. "And why does his head face backward? Does he have a crooked neck? There must be something wrong with him."

"Oh, he's okay," Aline said. "He's just smoothing his feathers with his bill." Loons do that to lock their feathers together and make them waterproof.

"Maybe," said Neil. "But he doesn't look right. I'm going to call him Crooked Neck."

Aline laughed. "That's a good name."

The two of them read until the sun sank low in the sky. Then Neil started the engine and they skimmed across the lake. They didn't know it yet, but their beloved loons now faced a different danger.

Like all loons, this one has red eyes. Red eyes help loons see better underwater.

Chapter 2

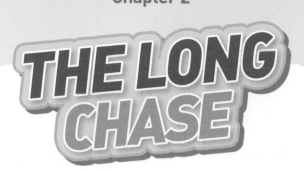

# THE LONG CHASE

The next day Neil suggested they go boating again. "I want to check on Crooked Neck," he told Aline.

It took a while to find the loon. And this time Crooked Neck was all alone. Chicks older than eight weeks can catch much of their own food. So their parents sometimes leave them alone during the day. But even his sibling had deserted him. And his head still faced backward!

"I knew it," Neil said. "Something is wrong with that bird."

The tone in his voice startled Aline. This time she had to agree. But what could be the matter?

Neil steered the boat in the bird's direction. A normal loon would have dived to get away from them. Crooked Neck didn't do that. But he zigzagged around so fast that they couldn't get close. Aline and Neil chased him all over the lake. After an hour, they gave up. They settled down and tried to read. This time Aline focused on an article she had printed off the Internet. And that's when it hit her.

"Neil," she said. "You're right. That loon is in trouble, and I think I know why!"

The piece she had read told about some people who were boating in the ocean. They came upon a whale. Imagine! An enormous sperm whale was just floating there, not moving. To their surprise, the boaters saw steam coming from its blowhole. They knew it was alive.

But why was it acting so strange? A closer look revealed that the whale was hopelessly tangled in a giant fishing net.

Aline suddenly realized that Crooked Neck must be tangled up, too. Only he was tangled in fishing line.

"What should we do?" Neil asked.

Aline pulled out her cell phone. "I'll call Gary Lee," she said. "He saved the loons last time, when their eggs were underwater."

But Gary wasn't home. His wife said he was out of town. Then she added something even more upsetting.

"Somebody called about that loon before. Gary tried to help, but he couldn't catch it."

"I can see why," groaned Neil when Aline told him. "Well, we can't wait. That poor loon is suffering something terrible. We'll have to help him ourselves."

"But how? We don't even have a net."

Neil didn't answer. He just restarted the engine and took off after the loon. He and Aline spent another two hours crisscrossing the lake. No matter how fast they drove, the speedy loon stayed out of reach. It was so frustrating.

"Stop swimming, you stupid loon!" Aline wanted to scream. "We're trying to help you." Finally, they lost heart.

"It's hopeless," Aline said. Neil shrugged in defeat and aimed the boat toward camp.

They were picking up speed when Aline turned for one last look. "Stop!" she yelled, springing to her feet. "Crooked Neck is here!"

"Here? Where?" Neil turned off the engine and ran to the back of the boat. He and Aline both peered over the side. Neither of them could believe what they saw. Crooked Neck had swum right up to them. He was almost close enough to touch. And sure enough, there was a green nylon fishing line trailing behind him.

"What changed his mind?" Aline wondered. "Why did he come to us?"

Neil shook his head in astonishment. "He must be getting weak. Maybe he saw us leaving and thought we were his last chance." Neil reached his hand back. "Quick. Give me the paddle."

Aline handed him the wooden canoe paddle they kept on the boat for emergencies. He stuck the paddle under the fishing line and lifted it up toward himself. Then he grabbed the line, dropped the paddle, and pulled in the loon. Once the loon was within reach, Neil grabbed his legs. Crooked Neck was upside down when Neil brought him into the boat. But Neil immediately shifted the loon to an upright position.

**Oooo hahahaha!**

What on earth? A loon suddenly rears up and flaps its wings. Then it runs on the water. Really! You might even hear its webbed feet slapping the water's surface. The crazy-acting bird also shrieks. It sounds like a wicked witch laughing.

Loons do this if anything—animal or human—comes close to their nest. They're trying to protect their eggs. These weird-sounding calls might not scare you in daytime. But a loon's cries can sound pretty spooky after dark.

Crooked Neck was scared now.
He nipped Neil on the back of his hand.
"Ouch!" he cried.

Had the loon bitten Aline, she probably
would have dropped it. But Neil grew up
on a farm. He had handled chickens.
He never let go.

Aline wrapped the bird in her beach
towel. Then she pinned him down on the
back seat so they could examine him.
What they saw made them feel sick.
The animal was tied up like a ball of
yarn. Green fishing line encircled his
legs, body, and one wing. He couldn't
move his head. His long, black beak
was tied shut with his tongue hanging
out one side. No way could he call
or eat!

How long had Crooked Neck been like this?

Neil dug out the cheese knife Aline had packed in their lunch. Aline held the bird down, while he sawed away at the tough nylon line. But the knife was too dull to make the cut.

"Keep a tight hold," Neil said. "We'll take the loon back to camp, where we have better tools." Neil returned to the driver's seat and started up the boat.

The wind blew Aline's hair as they shot across the water. Meanwhile, the loon flapped and squirmed beneath her hands. He was not fully grown. But he already weighed more than their cat. And he was strong.

"I can't hold him," Aline yelled. "He's going to get away!"

Neil Newman lifts Crooked Neck into the boat. The loon's head is tied to one side by fishing line.

## Chapter 3

# FREE AT LAST

It was a struggle, but somehow Aline hung onto the loon while Neil drove. They were zipping along when Neil spotted another boat up ahead. It had the word "Sheriff" painted on the side. Neil waved and headed straight for it. Once there, he cut the motor and the boat began rocking. Deputy Sheriff Russ Brombacher (sounds like BROM-bock-er) reached over and steadied it with his hands. That kept the two crafts from colliding. "What's the trouble?" Russ asked.

"Do you have a knife?" Neil said. "We have a loon wrapped up in fishing line. We need a sharp knife to cut him free."

Russ pulled a rope out of a storage bin and threw it to Neil. Neil used it to tie the two boats together. Then the deputy scrambled aboard. He handed Neil a folding knife with a broad, sharp blade. Neil nodded. "This will do it," he said.

Aline held the loon's body. The deputy held the bird's head. Neil slid the knife blade under a loop of line wrapped around the bird's beak. He sawed upward, being careful to avoid the loon's dried-out tongue. It looked brittle enough to break.

Neil finally removed the fishing line from around Crooked Neck's beak. But there was still a length of it hanging out of his throat. Neil tugged. More line came out. He tugged some more and line kept coming. It was like unwinding thread from a spool.

This all started with fishing line left in the lake. Maybe a fisherman baited his hook and cast his line, but his line broke. Or maybe his hook snagged. Unable to jerk it free, the fisherman cut off his line. Later a fish ate the bait. Now the fish was attached to the line. Then Crooked Neck ate the fish.

When Crooked Neck felt fishing line dangling from his mouth, he tried to get rid of it. He pointed his beak to the sky and flung his head around. But this only made things worse. The line wrapped around the loon's beak and wing. The more Crooked Neck struggled, the more tied up he got.

Neil kept pulling and two metal sinkers, or weights, emerged from deep inside the loon's belly. The last thing to come out was a rusty fishhook.

Aline turned the loon on his side and unwrapped the towel. Neil cut away the line from around the bird's wing. Untangling the loon had taken half an hour. But they did it. Crooked Neck was free! Neil scooped him up and tossed him over the side.

*Kersplash!* The loon hit the water. For a second, he just sat there. Then he turned his head to the left. He turned it to the right. He stretched his neck. It wasn't bent anymore. The excited loon flapped his wings and stood up on the water. *"Aaaaaaauhhhhhhhooooooooo!"* he wailed. The familiar call carried over the waves. But this time it sounded almost joyful. Was Crooked Neck telling his parents he was okay? Then he dived! And dived again! And dived some more!

The newly freed loon celebrated like a baseball player who had just won the World Series. Watching him brought tears of joy to Aline's eyes.

**Did You Know?**

**Loons can live to be 25 to 30 years old.**

Neil turned to the deputy. "Thank you," he said and shook his hand.

# Death Trap

This is the fishing line that caught Crooked Neck. It's made of nylon. If left in water, it will last 600 years. This bad stuff will clog up our lakes, rivers, and oceans. Countless waterbirds, turtles, and fish get caught in fishing line. Most of them will die.

But you can help. Buy biodegradable (sounds like bi-o-dih-GRADE-uh-bul) fishing line. It's made of corn! It rots away in only five years. Compare prices. Nylon line costs $5 a spool. A spool of biodegradable line costs $10. The good feeling you get from saving animals? That is worth millions!

Russ Brombacher grinned. "Glad I could help." He took back his knife and returned to his boat.

Aline and Neil felt like celebrating, too. They drove their boat around for an hour laughing and reliving their adventure. Then Neil asked, "Want to go back and see Crooked Neck again?"

"Yes!" Aline answered. They happily returned to where they had released the loon. But their spirits burst the moment they found him. Crooked Neck was in the one place a healthy loon should never be. He was sitting on shore! Loons avoid land because they can't walk well. They are much better at flying and swimming.

"Maybe we should catch him again and take him to a vet," Aline suggested.

Neil climbed out of the boat. His heart was heavy as he trudged barefoot through the sand. Then, surprise! The alert loon suddenly waddled to the water and swam away.

Neil beamed. "He's heading toward Dog Island," he said. "He's looking for his family."

It was Sunday night. Neil and Aline headed home as well. They had to work on Monday. But the next Saturday morning they took the boat back to check on their loon. The first time they circled the lake, Crooked Neck was nowhere to be found. The Newmans' thoughts turned gloomy. Was Crooked Neck still alive?

They started around again. And then they saw them. Their loons swam out of the marsh.

One, two, three . . . Aline sucked in her breath as she counted. There were four loons!

Neil reached over and squeezed Aline's hand. "So he did survive."

Crooked Neck would need to eat a lot to get as big as his sibling. But he had time. Nearly two months remained before the lake would freeze over. The only question still bothering Aline and Neil was whether Crooked Neck could handle food. Would his damaged tongue prevent him from eating?

They watched and waited. Then they saw something really special. One of

Crooked Neck's parents caught a fish . . . and gave it to him. Gulp! He sent it down the hatch.

Neil grinned and raised his hand in the air. "Mission accomplished," he said.

Aline grinned back and slapped him five. The happy feelings she had from helping that loon are still with her now.

THE END

Guess what? Aline Alexander Newman is not only the author of this book, she also took part in this story! Aline and her husband, Neil, helped save Crooked Neck from the fishing line in September of 2011.

# INDEX

# MORE INFORMATION

To find more information about the animal species featured in this book, check out these books, websites, and DVDs.

*National Geographic Kids Everything Big Cats,* National Geographic, 2011

*National Geographic Readers: Sea Turtles,* National Geographic, 2011

The Cornell Lab of Ornithology, "All About Birds: Common Loon," www.allaboutbirds.org/guide/Common_Loon/sounds

National Geographic, "Animals: Common Loon," animals.nationalgeographic.com/animals/birds/common-loon

National Geographic, "Animals: Green Sea Turtle," animals.nationalgeographic.com/animals/reptiles/green-turtle.html

National Geographic Kids, "Mammals: Clouded Leopards," video.nationalgeographic.com/video/kids/animals-pets-kids/mammals-kids/leopard-clouded-kids

Nat Geo Wild, "Return of the Clouded Leopards," DVD, 2013

This book is dedicated to the memory of my parents,
Howard and Phoebe Alexander,
who always believed I could do anything.

# CREDITS

Inside This Book TOC: Book 3, Lucky Leopards: leopard, ZSSD/Minden Pictures/National Geographic Creative; turtle, Isabellebonaire/Dreamstime; loon, Al Mueller/Shutterstock; Title page, pjmalsbury/iStockphoto; 4–5, © IFAW/WTI S. Kadur; 6, © IFAW/WTI A. Mookerjee; 15 (RT), © IFAW/WTI S. Kadur; 15 (LE), pjmalsbury/iStockphoto; 16, © IFAW/WTI A. Mookerjee; 22, Matt Gibson/Shutterstock; 26, ZSSD/ Minden Pictures National Geographic Creative; 35, © IFAW/WTI S. Kadur; 36–37, Nadine Fuller; 38, Jim Rice; 45, burcintuncer/iStockphoto; 48, Nadine Fuller; 54, Isabellebonaire/ Dreamstime; 58, richcarey/iStockphoto; 63, RonMasessa/iStockphoto; 68–69, PaulTessier/iStockphoto; 70, jimkruger/iStockphoto; 76, PaulTessier/ iStockphoto; 80, Al Mueller/Shutterstock; 87, Lynn_Bystrom/iStockphoto; 90, Aline A. Newman; 96, Aline A. Newman; 101, Lindsay Dancy-LDancy Design and Co-founder of Lilly Fund Boston, MA; 102, © David R. Lanteigne.

# ACKNOWLEDGMENTS

A special thank you to:

My husband, Neil, who helped me overcome a badly broken ankle to write this book

Ian Robinson and Sonali Ghosh, staunch defenders of clouded leopards and other wildlife

Nadine Fuller, Jim Rice, and James Burke, who rescued Koa and shared his story

Bob Zimmerman, Gary Lee, and Russ Brombacher, devoted Adirondackers and friends of loons

Hope Irvin Marston, Judy Ann Grant, Jule Lattimer, Jeanne Converse, and Jean Capron, past and present members of my writers' group

Regina Brooks, President of Serendipity Literary and my literary agent

The Old Forge Library and Isabella Worthen, Library Director, sponsors of 30-plus years of Old Forge Summer Writers Workshops

Marfé Ferguson Delano, eagle-eyed freelance project editor for National Geographic Children's Books

About the author: www.alinealexandernewman.com

# DON'T MISS!

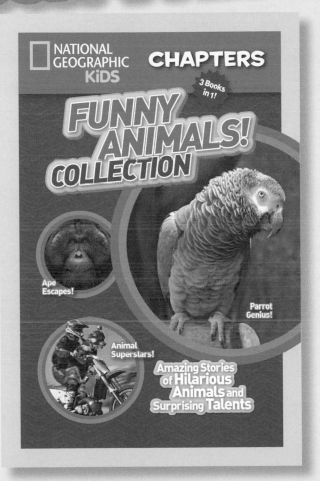

**NATIONAL GEOGRAPHIC KiDS** **CHAPTERS**

3 Books in 1!

FUNNY ANIMALS! COLLECTION

Ape Escapes!

Parrot Genius!

Animal Superstars!

Amazing Stories of **Hilarious** **Animals** and **Surprising Talents**

**Turn the page for a sneak preview . . .**

Tuna looks ready to sing for her favorite treat. That's tuna fish, of course!

# Born to PURR-FORM

## Spring 2003, Chicago, Illinois

A white kitten with big green eyes sat on a cardboard box. She looked very cute. Her name was Tuna. She had just been plopped down in a place she didn't know. Bright lights shone down from metal poles. They made her fur hot to the touch. A panting dog waited his turn in a corner. Tuna was having her picture taken.

"Most kittens would run," said Tuna's owner. Her name is Samantha Martin. Samantha loves cats. In fact, she loves all animals. She studied the care and raising of them in college. She dreamed of training animals for television and movies. When a photographer needed a kitten for a pet food ad, she offered her cat Tuna for the job. Now the photographer gripped a heavy camera and circled Tuna like a hungry wolf.

Samantha held her breath. *Please, Tuna,* she thought. *Don't bolt.*

The brave kitten stayed. She held her pose like a supermodel.

"Great!" the photographer said. "I got some good shots."

Samantha beamed. She opened a can of tuna fish, and the little kitty gobbled it up.

Before she got Tuna, Samantha trained rats. Her personal zoo also included a raccoon that could play basketball and a groundhog that could raise a flag. She had also trained a chicken, a duck, and a goose to play tiny musical instruments. But none of these acts drew a large enough audience for Samantha to earn a living from them.

To make it in show business, Samantha needed to train more popular animals. Watching Tuna in action started her thinking. Cat actors were much in demand. Somebody had to provide them. Why not Samantha?

"Tuna," Samantha said. "We're going to make you a star."

The next day Samantha brought out more tuna fish. She gave Tuna a nibble.

Then she waggled a long stick in front of her.

Tuna leaped and pounced, chasing the stick. The second Tuna's paw hit the stick, Samantha snapped a clicker. Then she gave the cat a bit of fish. They did this several times. Then, flash! Tuna realized that the click meant food. She had to touch the stick to get it.

The next day, Samantha brought out a push-button bell. Now she placed the stick on that. When Tuna touched the stick, she got nothing. She touched it again. Still nothing. Tuna scrunched her brow and twitched her tail. Maybe if she twirled around. *DING!* Tuna accidentally touched the bell. Samantha gave her a bit of fish. It took several lessons before Tuna figured out what Samantha wanted her to do.

Finally, Samantha gave Tuna a treat only if she actually rang the bell.

*DING! CLICK*. Treat!

Now Tuna knew her first trick.

The cat purred all through her training. *Hmm,* Samantha thought. *Tuna never used to purr. This must make her happy.* Most of the time Tuna was crabby. When Samantha picked her up, Tuna clawed to get down. If Samantha rubbed behind her ears, Tuna shook her head and walked away. But now Tuna came running when Samantha blew her training whistle. She quickly mastered trick after trick. "Tuna, you're brilliant," Samantha told her.

**Did You Know?**

**Nearly a third of U.S. households own at least one cat.**

But would Tuna perform for a crowd of people? There was one way to find out.

Samantha packed up Tuna's props. She wrote her name in glitter on the side of her pet carrier. Then she put Tuna inside and they left for California. They were going to a big fair where many pet lovers meet. Samantha could put Tuna's skills to the test there.

When they arrived at the fair, there were thousands of people strolling the grounds. Samantha lugged Tuna and her props through the crowd. She lugged them past a woolly poodle standing on a metal table. She lugged them past row upon row of big, heavy fish tanks. She lugged them past hamsters snoozing in metal cages. Samantha ignored them all. She needed to find the perfect spot for Tuna to perform.

# Kitty "High Five"

You can train your cat to high-five. Ask your parents to buy a clicker and a bag of kitty treats at the pet store. Then sit on the floor with your cat. Hold the clicker in one hand. Grasp a treat between the fingers of your other hand. Now jiggle the treat in front of your cat. The second he swats for it, click and give him the treat. Do this over and over. Soon your kitty will slap you five whenever you click, even without a treat.

Aha! Samantha spied an empty countertop. She set Tuna's carrier down and called out to people walking past. "Hey!" she shouted. "Check out my cat. My cat needs a job."

A small crowd gathered. Samantha opened the pet carrier door and lured Tuna out with her favorite treat. The tricky kitty ignored all the people. She rang her bell. She rolled over. She jumped through a hoop. The crowd laughed and clapped, and Samantha grinned. What a cat! Tuna had what it takes. Maybe they would get lucky. Maybe Tuna would be discovered and become an actor.

Instead, a dog appeared.

**Did You Know?**

**Like dogs, cats sweat through their paws.**

Tuna froze. How dare this big mutt invade her space! Before Samantha could stop her, the cat leaped onto the dog's back. *EEEYOW!* She dug in her claws.

The dog whirled. Tuna screeched.

Fur flew as Samantha stood there in shock. Then as suddenly as everything started, it stopped. The fearless Tuna jumped back on the counter. Samantha stuffed her into her carrier and shut the door. The dog owner yanked his animal away.

After that Samantha put Tuna on a leash. She scheduled shows at libraries, schools, and birthday parties. These would not pay much. But at least Tuna would get some practice. Samantha prayed that their big break would come soon.

Head down, paws tucked in, Tuna soars over the hurdles.

## Chapter 2

# Lights, Camera, ACTION!

**T**una loved performing, but it cost a lot of money to travel to shows. Samantha couldn't earn much at other jobs because Tuna took up almost all her time. Samantha didn't know how much longer she could keep it up. Then one day, she got an exciting phone call.

"I found your number on the Internet," the speaker said. "I'm looking for a cat actor." The voice belonged to a college student in Florida named Dana Buning. Dana was making a short movie for a class assignment. It was a scary movie called *Zeke* (sounds like ZEEK). It starred a man and his cat.

"Are you paying?" Samantha asked.

"Yes. We have a production budget," said Dana.

"We'll do it!" Samantha said with joy.

"Not so fast," Dana said. "Four other cats are trying out for the part. I need to see what Tuna can do."

Dana sent Samantha the script. Tuna was to play the bad guy. First off she had to look angry. That was easy. Tuna was naturally cranky. But she also needed to lick her mouth on cue. She had to snarl and pretend to bite. She had to lie flat on her back with her front legs stretched over her head. She needed to stay that way while other actors performed around her.

Samantha didn't know if Tuna would be okay sitting still for a big, scary camera on wheels. This role needed a brave cat.

Samantha decided that they would go for it. She taught Tuna to do everything the film needed. Tuna caught on fast.

Soon it was time to show the world Tuna's new tricks. Samantha had her perform for free to get her used to acting in strange places. The more shows Tuna did, the braver she got. Samantha recorded the shows and sent the videos to Florida. Dana studied them carefully. One day she called Samantha.

Yippee! Tuna got the part!

"The other cats are too nice," Dana said. "We like Tuna because she looks evil."

Two trips to Florida followed. Tuna worked hard. When the movie was done, she appeared in almost every scene.

Samantha was proud of her cat. She expected to hear from Hollywood any day.

But months passed and the phone didn't ring. "Don't worry, Tuna," Samantha said. "You'll get your chance. Just wait and see."

Tuna just blinked.

Samantha started taking the cat to a monthly film festival. She handed out flyers and set up a folding table to showcase Tuna. Sometimes show business people attended these movies. Maybe one of them would need a cat actor and Tuna would land another movie role.

In the meantime, Samantha taught Tuna to pluck a tiny guitar. One night, Samantha took the cat to a dinner theater. Dishes were clattering. People were talking. A hired band was playing in the next room. Samantha wondered if Tuna would perform.

But when she opened Tuna's carrier, hooray! The furry musician ran straight to her guitar. Tuna played like she was the only performer in the place.

Samantha had an idea. *I'll form an all-cat band,* she decided. She already had tiny instruments left over from her goose, duck, and chicken act. All she had to do was train some more cats to play them.

**Did You Know?**

In ancient Egypt, cats were made into mummies after they died.

The trouble was that Samantha's new cats were not like Tuna. Dakota, Pinky, and Nue jammed it up big time at home. But take them out in public? The scaredy-cats hid in their carriers.

Samantha wondered why the cats were so afraid. What could she do to make them feel safe? She tried offering different treats. That didn't work. Maybe she should ditch the band and form a duo with Tuna and just one other cat. That didn't work either.

Somehow Samantha had to make different performance spaces feel the same. Finally, she had an idea. She bought a sheet of soft vinyl (sounds like VINE-el) floor covering. At home she laid it out on her kitchen table and set up the band instruments on top. The cats got used to feeling the soft plastic under their feet.

When Samantha did a show, she rolled up the floor and took it with her.

Now the floor felt the same wherever they went. "They step on that," Samantha said, "and everything is okay."

One night she placed an ad on the Internet. "I have a Cat Circus act," she typed. "We need a place to perform."

A few days later, Samantha turned on her computer and bingo! A local art gallery was offering her space. She brought the roll of vinyl flooring and a cloth backdrop. The cats felt at home and played like rock stars.

**Want to know what happens next? Be sure to check out the *Funny Animals! Collection***

# CREDITS

3, © Steve Grubman; 10, Linn Currie/Shutterstock; 13, Courtesy Samantha Martin; 21, © Steve Grubman.